Hippolytus by Euripides

Euripides is rightly lauded as one of the great dramatists of all time. In his lifetime, he wrote over 90 plays and although only 18 have survived they reveal the scope and reach of his genius.

Euripides is identified with many theatrical innovations that have influenced drama all the way down to modern times, especially in the representation of traditional, mythical heroes as ordinary people in extraordinary circumstances.

As would be expected from a life lived 2,500 years ago, details of it are few and far between. Accounts of his life, written down the ages, do exist but whether much is reliable or surmised is open to debate.

Most accounts agree that he was born on Salamis Island around 480 BC, to mother Cleito and father Mnesarchus, a retailer who lived in a village near Athens. Upon the receipt of an oracle saying that his son was fated to win "crowns of victory", Mnesarchus insisted that the boy should train for a career in athletics.

However, what is clear is that athletics was not to be the way to win crowns of victory. Euripides had been lucky enough to have been born in the era as the other two masters of Greek Tragedy; Sophocles and Æschylus. It was in their footsteps that he was destined to follow.

His first play was performed some thirteen years after the first of Socrates plays and a mere three years after Æschylus had written his classic The Oristria.

Theatre was becoming a very important part of the Greek culture. The Dionysia, held annually, was the most important festival of theatre and second only to the fore-runner of the Olympic games, the Panathenia, held every four years, in appeal.

Euripides first competed in the City Dionysia, in 455 BC, one year after the death of Æschylus, and, incredibly, it was not until 441 BC that he won first prize. His final competition in Athens was in 408 BC. The Bacchae and Iphigenia in Aulis were performed after his death in 405 BC and first prize was awarded posthumously. Altogether his plays won first prize only five times.

Euripides was also a great lyric poet. In Medea, for example, he composed for his city, Athens, "the noblest of her songs of praise". His lyric skills however are not just confined to individual poems: "A play of Euripides is a musical whole....one song echoes motifs from the preceding song, while introducing new ones."

Much of his life and his whole career coincided with the struggle between Athens and Sparta for hegemony in Greece but he didn't live to see the final defeat of his city.

Euripides fell out of favour with his fellow Athenian citizens and retired to the court of Archelaus, king of Macedon, who treated him with consideration and affection.

At his death, in around 406BC, he was mourned by the king, who, refusing the request of the Athenians that his remains be carried back to the Greek city, buried him with much splendor within his own dominions. His tomb was placed at the confluence of two streams, near Arethusa in Macedonia, and a cenotaph was built to his memory on the road from Athens towards the Piraeus.

Index of Contents

INTRODUCTORY NOTE

Euripides, the youngest of the trio of great Greek tragedians was born at Salamis in 480 B.C., on the day when the Greeks won their momentous naval victory there over the fleet of the Persians. The precise social status of his parents is not clear but he received a good education, was early distinguished as an athlete, and showed talent in painting and oratory. He was a fellow student of Pericles, and his dramas show the influence of the philosophical ideas of Anaxagoras and of Socrates, with whom he was personally intimate. Like Socrates, he was accused of impiety, and this, along with domestic infelicity, has been supposed to afford a motive for his withdrawal from Athens, first to Magnesia and later to the court of Anchelaüs in Macedonia where he died in 406 B.C.

The first tragedy of Euripides was produced when he was about twenty-five, and he was several times a victor in the tragic contests. In spite of the antagonisms which he aroused and the criticisms which were hurled upon him in, for example, the comedies of Aristophanes, he attained a very great popularity; and Plutarch tells that those Athenians who were taken captive in the disastrous Sicilian expedition of 413 B.C. were offered freedom by their captors if they could recite from the works of Euripides. Of the hundred and twenty dramas ascribed to Euripides, there have come down to us complete eighteen tragedies and one satyric drama, "Cyclops," beside numerous fragments.

The works of Euripides are generally regarded as showing the beginning of the decline of Greek tragedy. The idea of Fate hitherto dominant in the plays of his predecessors, tends to be degraded by him into mere chance; the characters lose much of their ideal quality; and even gods and heroes are represented as moved by the petty motives of ordinary humanity. The chorus is often quite detached from the action; the poetry is florid; and the action is frequently tinged with sensationalism. In spite of all this, Euripides remains a great poet; and his picturesqueness and tendencies to what are now called realism and romanticism, while marking his inferiority to the chaste classicism of Sophocles, bring him more easily within the sympathetic interest of the modern reader.

THE PERSONS
THE GODDESS APHRODITE
THESEUS, King of Athens and Trozên

PHAEDRA, daughter of Minos, King of Crete, wife to Theseus
HIPPOLYTUS, bastard son of Theseus and the Amazon Hippolyte
THE NURSE OF PHAEDRA
A HENCHMAN OF HIPPOLYTUS
THE GODDESS ARTEMIS
AN OLD HUNTSMAN
A CHORUS OF HUNTSMEN
ATTENDANTS ON THE THREE ROYAL PERSONS
A CHORUS OF TROZENIAN WOMEN, WITH THEIR LEADER

Trozên.

The play was first acted when Epameinon was Archon, Olympiad 87, year 4 (B.C. 429). Euripides was first, Iophon second, Ion third.

APHRODITE
Great among men, and not unnamed am I,
The Cyprian, in God's inmost halls on high.
And wheresoe'er from Pontus to the far
Red West men dwell, and see the glad day-star,
And worship Me, the pious heart I bless,
And wreck that life that lives in stubbornness.
For that there is, even in a great God's mind,
That hungereth for the praise of human kind.

So runs my word; and soon the very deed
Shall follow. For this Prince of Theseus' seed,
Hippolytus, child of that dead Amazon,
And reared by saintly Pittheus in his own
Strait ways, hath dared, alone of all Trozên,
To hold me least of spirits and most mean,
And spurns my spell and seeks no woman's kiss,
But great Apollo's sister, Artemis,
He holds of all most high, gives love and praise,
And through the wild dark woods for ever strays,
He and the Maid together, with swift hounds
To slay all angry beasts from out these bounds,
To more than mortal friendship consecrate!

I grudge it not. No grudge know I, nor hate;
Yet, seeing he hath offended, I this day
Shall smite Hippolytus. Long since my way

Was opened, nor needs now much labour more.

For once from Pittheus' castle to the shore
Of Athens came Hippolytus over-seas
Seeking the vision of the Mysteries.
And Phaedra there, his father's Queen high-born;
Saw him, and as she saw, her heart was torn
With great love, by the working of my will.
And for his sake, long since, on Pallas' hill,
Deep in the rock, that Love no more might roam,
She built a shrine, and named it Love-at-home:
And the rock held it, but its face alway
Seeks Trozên o'er the seas. Then came the day
When Theseus, for the blood of kinsmen shed,
Spake doom of exile on himself, and fled,
Phaedra beside him, even to this Trozên.
And here that grievous and amazed Queen,
Wounded and wondering, with ne'er a word,
Wastes slowly; and her secret none hath heard
Nor dreamed.

But never thus this love shall end!
To Theseus' ear some whisper will I send,
And all be bare! And that proud Prince, my foe,
His sire shall slay with curses. Even so
Endeth that boon the great Lord of the Main
To Theseus gave, the Three Prayers not in vain.

And she, not in dishonour, yet shall die.
I would not rate this woman's pain so high
As not to pay mine haters in full fee
That vengeance that shall make all well with me.

But soft, here comes he, striding from the chase,
Our Prince Hippolytus!—I will go my ways.—
And hunters at his heels: and a loud throng
Glorying Artemis with praise and song!
Little he knows that Hell's gates opened are,
And this his last look on the great Day-star!

[APHRODITE withdraws, unseen by **HIPPOLYTUS** and a band of **HUNTSMEN**, who enter from the left,
singing. They pass the Statue of **APHRODITE** without notice.

HIPPOLYTUS
Follow, O follow me,
Singing on your ways
Her in whose hand are we,
Her whose own flock we be,
The Zeus-Child, the Heavenly;
To Artemis be praise!

HUNTSMAN

Hail to thee, Maiden blest,
Proudest and holiest:
God's Daughter, great in bliss,
Leto-born, Artemis!
Hail to thee, Maiden, far
Fairest of all that are,
Yea, and most high thine home,
Child of the Father's hall;
Hear, O most virginal,
Hear, O most fair of all,
In high God's golden dome.

[The **HUNTSMEN** have gathered about the altar of **ARTEMIS**. **HIPPOLYTUS** now advances from them, and approaches the Statue with a wreath in his hand.

HIPPOLYTUS

To thee this wreathed garland, from a green
And virgin meadow bear I, O my Queen,
Where never shepherd leads his grazing ewes
Nor scythe has touched. Only the river dews
Gleam, and the spring bee sings, and in the glade
Hath Solitude her mystic garden made.
No evil hand may cull it: only he
Whose heart hath known the heart of Purity,
Unlearned of man, and true whate'er befall.
Take therefore from pure hands this coronal,
O mistress loved, thy golden hair to twine.
For, sole of living men, this grace is mine,
To dwell with thee, and speak, and hear replies
Of voice divine, though none may see thine eyes.
Oh, keep me to the end in this same road!

[An **OLD HUNTSMAN**, who has stood apart from the rest, here comes up to **HIPPOLYTUS**.

HUNTSMAN

My Prince—for "Master" name I none but God—
Gave I good counsel, wouldst thou welcome it?

HIPPOLYTUS

Right gladly, friend; else were I poor of wit.

HUNTSMAN

Knowest thou one law, that through the world has won?

HIPPOLYTUS

What wouldst thou? And how runs thy law? Say on.

HUNTSMAN

It hates that Pride that speaks not all men fair!

HIPPOLYTUS
And rightly.   Pride breeds hatred everywhere.

HUNTSMAN
And good words love, and grace in all men's sight?

HIPPOLYTUS
Aye, and much gain withal, for trouble slight.

HUNTSMAN
How deem'st thou of the Gods? Are they the same?

HIPPOLYTUS
Surely: we are but fashioned on their frame.

HUNTSMAN
Why then wilt thou be proud, and worship not ...

HIPPOLYTUS
Whom? If the name be speakable, speak out!

HUNTSMAN
She stands here at thy gate: the Cyprian Queen!

HIPPOLYTUS
I greet her from afar: my life is clean.

HUNTSMAN
Clean? Nay, proud, proud; a mark for all to scan!

HIPPOLYTUS
Each mind hath its own bent, for God or man.

HUNTSMAN
God grant thee happiness ... and wiser thought!

HIPPOLYTUS
These Spirits that reign in darkness like me not.

HUNTSMAN
What the Gods ask, O Son, that man must pay!

HIPPOLYTUS [Turning from him to the others]
On, huntsmen, to the Castle! Make your way
Straight to the feast room; 'tis a merry thing
After the chase, a board of banqueting.
And see the steeds be groomed, and in array
The chariot dight. I drive them forth to-day

[He pauses, and makes a slight gesture of reverence to the Statue on the left. Then to the OLD
HUNTSMAN.

That for thy Cyprian, friend, and nought beside!

[**HIPPOLYTUS** follows the huntsmen, who stream by the central door in the Castle. The OLD
HUNTSMAN remains.

HUNTSMAN [Approaching the Statue and kneeling]
O Cyprian—for a young man in his pride
I will not follow!—here before thee, meek,
In that one language that a slave may speak,
I pray thee; Oh, if some wild heart in froth
Of youth surges against thee, be not wroth
For ever! Nay, be far and hear not then:
Gods should be gentler and more wise than men!

[He rises and follows the **OTHERS** into the Castle.

[The Orchestra is empty for a moment, then there enter from right and left several Trosenian
WOMEN young and old. Their number eventually amounts to fifteen.

CHORUS
There riseth a rock-born river,
Of Ocean's tribe, men say;
The crags of it gleam and quiver,
And pitchers dip in the spray:
A woman was there with raiment white
To bathe and spread in the warm sunlight,
And she told a tale to me there by the river
The tale of the Queen and her evil day:

How, ailing beyond allayment,
Within she hath bowed her head,
And with shadow of silken raiment
The bright brown hair bespread.
For three long days she hath lain forlorn,
Her lips untainted of flesh or corn,
For that secret sorrow beyond allayment
That steers to the far sad shore of the dead.

SOME WOMEN
Is this some Spirit, O child of man?
Doth Hecat hold thee perchance, or Pan?
Doth she of the Mountains work her ban,
Or the dread Corybantes bind thee?

OTHERS
Nay, is it sin that upon thee lies,
Sin of forgotten sacrifice,
In thine own Dictynna's sea-wild eyes?
Who in Limna here can find thee;
For the Deep's dry floor is her easy way,

And she moves in the salt wet whirl of the spray.

OTHER WOMEN
Or doth the Lord of Erechtheus' race,
Thy Theseus, watch for a fairer face,
For secret arms in a silent place,
Far from thy love or chiding?

OTHERS
Or hath there landed, amid the loud
Hum of Piraeus' sailor-crowd,
Some Cretan venturer, weary-browed,
Who bears to the Queen some tiding;
Some far home-grief, that hath bowed her low,
And chained her soul to a bed of woe?

AN OLDER WOMAN
Nay—know yet not?—this burden hath alway lain
On the devious being of woman; yea, burdens twain,
The burden of Wild Will and the burden of Pain.
Through my heart once that wind of terror sped;
But I, in fear confessèd,
Cried from the dark to Her in heavenly bliss,
The Helper of Pain, the Bow-Maid Artemis:
Whose feet I praise for ever, where they tread
Far off among the blessèd!

THE LEADER
But see, the Queen's grey nurse at the door,
Sad-eyed and sterner, methinks, than of yore
With the Queen. Doth she lead her hither
To the wind and sun?—Ah, fain would I know
What strange betiding hath blanched that brow
And made that young life wither.

[The **NURSE** comes out from the central door followed by **PHAEDRA**, who is supported by **TWO HANDMAIDS**. They make ready a couch for **PHAEDRA** to lie upon.

NURSE
O sick and sore are the days of men!
What wouldst thou? What shall I change again
Here is the Sun for thee; here is the sky;
And thy weary pillows wind-swept lie,
By the castle door.
But the cloud of thy brow is dark, I ween;
And soon thou wilt back to thy bower within:
So swift to change is the path of thy feet,
And near things hateful, and far things sweet;
So was it before!

Oh, pain were better than tending pain!

For that were single, and this is twain,
With grief of heart and labour of limb.
Yet all man's life is but ailing and dim,
And rest upon earth comes never.
But if any far-off state there be,
Dearer than life to mortality;
The hand of the Dark hath hold thereof,
And mist is under and mist above.
And so we are sick of life, and cling
On earth to this nameless and shining thing.
For other life is a fountain sealed,
And the deeps below are unrevealed,
And we drift on legends for ever!

[**PHAEDRA** during this has been laid on her couch; she speaks to the **HANDMAIDS**.

PHAEDRA
Yes; lift me: not my head so low.
There, hold my arms.—Fair arms they seem!—
My poor limbs scarce obey me now!
Take off that hood that weighs my brow,
And let my long hair stream.

NURSE
Nay, toss not, Child, so feveredly.
The sickness best will win relief
By quiet rest and constancy.
All men have grief.

PHAEDRA [Not noticing her]
Oh for a deep and dewy spring,
With runlets cold to draw and drink!
And a great meadow blossoming,
Long-grassed, and poplars in a ring,
To rest me by the brink!

NURSE
Nay, Child! Shall strangers hear this tone
So wild, and thoughts so fever-flown?

PHAEDRA
Oh, take me to the Mountain! Oh,
Pass the great pines and through the wood,
Up where the lean hounds softly go,
A-whine for wild things' blood,
And madly flies the dappled roe.
O God, to shout and speed them there,
An arrow by my chestnut hair
Drawn tight, and one keen glimmering spear—
Ah! if I could!

NURSE

What wouldst thou with them—fancies all!—
Thy hunting and thy fountain brink?
What wouldst thou? By the city wall
Canst hear our own brook plash and fall
Downhill, if thou wouldst drink.

PHAEDRA

O Mistress of the Sea-lorn Mere
Where horse-hoofs beat the sand and sing,
O Artemis, that I were there
To tame Enetian steeds and steer
Swift chariots in the ring!

NURSE

Nay, mountainward but now thy hands
Yearned out, with craving for the chase;
And now toward the unseaswept sands
Thou roamest, where the coursers pace!
O wild young steed, what prophet knows
The power that holds thy curb, and throws
Thy swift heart from its race?

[At these words **PHAEDRA** gradually recovers herself and pays attention.

PHAEDRA

What have I said? Woe's me! And where
Gone straying from my wholesome mind?
What? Did I fall in some god's snare?
—Nurse, veil my head again, and blind
Mine eyes.—There is a tear behind
That lash.—Oh, I am sick with shame!
Aye, but it hath a sting,
To come to reason; yet the name
Of madness is an awful thing.—
Could I but die in one swift flame
Unthinking, unknowing!

NURSE

I veil thy face, Child.—Would that so
Mine own were veiled for evermore,
So sore I love thee! ... Though the lore
Of long life mocks me, and I know
How love should be a lightsome thing
Not rooted in the deep o' the heart;
With gentle ties, to twine apart
If need so call, or closer cling.—
Why do I love thee so? O fool,
O fool, the heart that bleeds for twain,
And builds, men tell us, walls of pain,
To walk by love's unswerving rule

The same for ever, stern and true!
For "Thorough" is no word of peace:
'Tis "Naught-too-much" makes trouble cease.
And many a wise man bows thereto.

[The **LEADER OF THE CHORUS** here approaches the **NURSE**.

LEADER
Nurse of our Queen, thou watcher old and true,
We see her great affliction, but no clue
Have we to learn the sickness. Wouldst thou tell
The name and sort thereof, 'twould like us well.

NURSE
Small leechcraft have I, and she tells no man.

LEADER
Thou know'st no cause? Nor when the unrest began?

NURSE
It all comes to the same. She will not speak.

LEADER [Turning and looking at **PHAEDRA**]
How she is changed and wasted! And how weak!

NURSE
'Tis the third day she hath fasted utterly.

LEADER
What, is she mad? Or doth she seek to die?

NURSE
I know not. But to death it sure must lead.

LEADER
'Tis strange that Theseus takes hereof no heed.

NURSE
She hides her wound, and vows it is not so.

LEADER
Can he not look into her face and know?

NURSE
Nay, he is on a journey these last days.

LEADER
Canst thou not force her, then? Or think of ways
To trap the secret of the sick heart's pain?

NURSE

Have I not tried all ways, and all in vain?
Yet will I cease not now, and thou shalt tell
If in her grief I serve my mistress well!

[She goes across to where **PHAEDRA** lies; and presently, while speaking, kneels by her.

Dear daughter mine, all that before was said
Let both of us forget; and thou instead
Be kindlier, and unlock that prisoned brow.
And I, who followed then the wrong road, now
Will leave it and be wiser. If thou fear
Some secret sickness, there be women here
To give thee comfort.

[**PHAEDRA** shakes her head.

No; not secret? Then
Is it a sickness meet for aid of men?
Speak, that a leech may tend thee.
Silent still?
Nay, Child, what profits silence? If 'tis ill
This that I counsel, makes me see the wrong:
If well, then yield to me.
Nay, Child, I long
For one kind word, one look!

[**PHAEDRA** lies motionless. The **NURSE** rises.

Oh, woe is me!
Women, we labour here all fruitlessly,
All as far off as ever from her heart!
She ever scorned me, and now hears no part
Of all my prayers!

[Turning to **PHAEDRA** again.

Nay, hear thou shalt, and be,
If so thou will, more wild than the wild sea;
But know, thou art thy little ones' betrayer!
If thou die now, shall child of thine be heir
To Theseus' castle? Nay, not thine, I ween,
But hers! That barbèd Amazonian Queen
Hath left a child to bend thy children low,
A bastard royal-hearted—sayst not so?—
Hippolytus...

PHAEDRA
Ah!

[She starts up, sitting, and throws the veil off.

NURSE
That stings thee?

PHAEDRA
Nurse, most sore
Thou hast hurt me! In God's name, speak that name no more.

NURSE
Thou seest? Thy mind is clear; but with thy mind
Thou wilt not save thy children, nor be kind
To thine own life.

PHAEDRA
My children? Nay, most dear
I love them,—Far, far other grief is here.

NURSE [After a pause, wondering]
Thy hand is clean, O Child, from stain of blood?

PHAEDRA
My hand is clean; but is my heart, O God?

NURSE
Some enemy's spell hath made thy spirit dim?

PHAEDRA
He hates me not that slays me, nor I him.

NURSE
Theseus, the King, hath wronged thee in man's wise?

PHAEDRA
Ah, could but I stand guiltless in his eyes!

NURSE
O speak! What is this death-fraught mystery?

PHAEDRA
Nay, leave me to my wrong. I wrong not thee.

NURSE [Suddenly throwing herself in supplication at **PHAEDRA**'S feet
Not wrong me, whom thou wouldst all desolate leave?

PHAEDRA [Rising and trying to move away]
What wouldst thou? Force me? Clinging to my sleeve?

NURSE
Yea, to thy knees; and weep; and let not go!

PHAEDRA
Woe to thee, Woman, if thou learn it, woe!

NURSE
I know no bitterer woe than losing thee.

PHAEDRA
Yet the deed shall honour me.

NURSE
Why hide what honours thee? 'Tis all I claim!

PHAEDRA
Why, so I build up honour out of shame!

NURSE
Then speak, and higher still thy fame shall stand.

PHAEDRA
Go, in God's name!—Nay, leave me; loose my hand!

NURSE
Never, until thou grant me what I pray.

PHAEDRA [Yielding, after a pause]
So be it. I dare not tear that hand away.

NURSE [Rising and releasing **PHAEDRA**]
Tell all thou wilt, Daughter. I speak no more.

PHAEDRA [After a long pause]
Mother, poor Mother, that didst love so sore!

NURSE
What mean'st thou, Child? The Wild Bull of the Tide?

PHAEDRA
And thou, sad sister, Dionysus' bride!

NURSE
Child! wouldst thou shame the house where thou wast born?

PHAEDRA
And I the third, sinking most all-forlorn!

NURSE [To herself]
I am all lost and feared. What will she say?

PHAEDRA
From there my grief comes, not from yesterday.

NURSE
I come no nearer to thy parable.

PHAEDRA
Oh, would that thou could'st tell what I must tell!

NURSE
I am no seer in things I wot not of.

PHAEDRA [Again hesitating]
What is it that they mean, who say men...love?

NURSE
A thing most sweet, my Child, yet dolorous.

PHAEDRA
Only the half, belike, hath fallen on us!

NURSE [Starting]
On thee? Love?—Oh, what say'st thou? What man's son?

PHAEDRA
What man's? There was a Queen, an Amazon ...

NURSE
Hippolytus, say'st thou?

PHAEDRA [Again wrapping her face in the veil]
Nay, 'twas thou, not I!

[**PHAEDRA** sinks back on the couch and covers her face again. The **NURSE** starts violently from her and walks up and down.

NURSE
O God! what wilt thou say, Child? Wouldst thou try
To kill me?—Oh, 'tis more than I can bear;
Women. I will no more of it, this glare
Of hated day, this shining of the sky.
I will fling down my body, and let it lie
Till life be gone!
Women, God rest with you,
My works are over! For the pure and true
Are forced to evil, against their own heart's vow,
And love it!

[She suddenly sees the Statue of **CYPRIS**, and stands with her eyes riveted upon it.

Ah, Cyprian! No god art thou,
But more than god, and greater, that hath thrust
Me and my queen and all our house to dust!

[She throws herself on the ground close to the statue.

CHORUS
SOME WOMEN
O Women, have ye heard? Nay, dare ye hear
The desolate cry of the young Queen's misery?

A WOMAN
My Queen, I love thee dear,
Yet liefer were I dead than framed like thee.

OTHERS
Woe, woe to me for this thy bitter bane,
Surely the food man feeds upon is pain!

OTHERS
How wilt thou bear thee through this livelong day,
Lost, and thine evil naked to the light?
Strange things are close upon us—who shall say
How strange?—save one thing that is plain to sight,
The stroke of the Cyprian and the fall thereof
On thee, thou child of the Isle of fearful Love!

[**PHAEDRA** during this has risen from the couch and comes forward collectedly. As she speaks the **NURSE** gradually rouses herself, and listens more calmly.

PHAEDRA
O Women, dwellers in this portal-seat
Of Pelops' land, gazing towards my Crete,
How oft, in other days than these, have I
Through night's long hours thought of man's misery,
And how this life is wrecked! And, to mine eyes,
Not in man's knowledge, not in wisdom, lies
The lack that makes for sorrow. Nay, we scan
And know the right—for wit hath many a man—
But will not to the last end strive and serve.
For some grow too soon weary, and some swerve
To other paths, setting before the Right
The diverse far-off image of Delight:
And many are delights beneath the sun!
Long hours of converse; and to sit alone
Musing—a deadly happiness!—and Shame:
Though two things there be hidden in one name,
And Shame can be slow poison if it will;

This is the truth I saw then, and see still;
Nor is there any magic that can stain
That white truth for me, or make me blind again.
Come, I will show thee how my spirit hath moved.
When the first stab came, and I knew I loved,
I cast about how best to face mine ill.
And the first thought that came, was to be still
And hide my sickness.—For no trust there is

In man's tongue, that so well admonishes
And counsels and betrays, and waxes fat
With griefs of its own gathering!—After that
I would my madness bravely bear, and try
To conquer by mine own heart's purity.

My third mind, when these two availed me naught
To quell love was to die—

[Motion of protest among the **WOMEN**.

—the best, best thought—
—Gainsay me not—of all that man can say!
I would not have mine honour hidden away;
Why should I have my shame before men's eyes
Kept living? And I knew, in deadly wise,
Shame was the deed and shame the suffering;
And I a woman, too, to face the thing,
Despised of all!

Oh, utterly accurst
Be she of women, whoso dared the first
To cast her honour out to a strange man!
'Twas in some great house, surely, that began
This plague upon us; then the baser kind,
When the good led towards evil, followed blind
And joyous! Cursed be they whose lips are clean
And wise and seemly, but their hearts within
Rank with bad daring! How can they, O Thou
That walkest on the waves, great Cyprian, how
Smile in their husbands' faces, and not fall,
Not cower before the Darkness that knows all,
Aye, dread the dead still chambers, lest one day
The stones find voice, and all be finished!
Nay,
Friends, 'tis for this I die; lest I stand there
Having shamed my husband and the babes I bare.
In ancient Athens they shall some day dwell,
My babes, free men, free-spoken, honourable,

EURIPIDES
And when one asks their mother, proud of me!
For, oh, it cows a man, though bold he be,
To know a mother's or a father's sin.

'Tis written, one way is there, one, to win
This life's race, could man keep it from his birth,
A true clean spirit. And through all this earth
To every false man, that hour comes apace
When Time holds up a mirror to his face,
And girl-like, marvelling, there he stares to see

How foul his heart! Be it not so with me!

LEADER OF CHORUS
Ah, God, how sweet is virtue, and how wise,
And honour its due meed in all men's eyes!

NURSE [Who has now risen and recovered herself]
Mistress, a sharp swift terror struck me low
A moment since, hearing of this thy woe.
But now—I was a coward! And men say
Our second thought the wiser is alway.

This is no monstrous thing; no grief too dire
To meet with quiet thinking. In her ire
A most strong goddess hath swept down on thee.
Thou lovest. Is that so strange? Many there be
Beside thee! ... And because thou lovest, wilt fall
And die! And must all lovers die, then? All
That are or shall be? A blithe law for them!
Nay, when in might she swoops, no strength can stem
Cypris; and if man yields him, she is sweet;
But is he proud and stubborn? From his feet
She lifts him, and—how think you?—flings to scorn!

She ranges with the stars of eve and morn,
She wanders in the heaving of the sea,
And all life lives from her.—Aye, this is she
That sows Love's seed and brings Love's fruit to birth;
And great Love's brethren are all we on earth!

Nay, they who con grey books of ancient days
Or dwell among the Muses, tell—and praise—
How Zeus himself once yearned for Semelê;
How maiden Eôs in her radiancy
Swept Kephalos to heaven away, away,
For sore love's sake. And there they dwell, men say,
And fear not, fret not; for a thing too stern
Hath met and crushed them!

And must thou, then, turn
And struggle? Sprang there from thy father's blood
Thy little soul all lonely? Or the god
That rules thee, is he other than our gods?
Nay, yield thee to men's ways, and kiss their rods!
How many, deem'st thou, of men good and wise
Know their own home's blot, and avert their eyes?
How many fathers, when a son has strayed
And toiled beneath the Cyprian, bring him aid,
Not chiding? And man's wisdom e'er hath been
To keep what is not good to see, unseen!

A straight and perfect life is not for man;
Nay, in a shut house, let him, if he can,
'Mid sheltered rooms, make all lines true. But here,
Out in the wide sea fallen, and full of fear,
Hopest thou so easily to swim to land?

Canst thou but set thine ill days on one hand
And more good days on the other, verily,
O child of woman, life is well with thee!

[She pauses, and then draws nearer to **PHAEDRA**.

Nay, dear my daughter, cease thine evil mind,
Cease thy fierce pride! For pride it is, and blind,
To seek to outpass gods!—Love on and dare:
A god hath willed it! And, since pain is there,
Make the pain sleep! Songs are there to bring calm,
And magic words. And I shall find the balm,
Be sure, to heal thee. Else in sore dismay
Were men, could not we women find our way!

LEADER OF THE CHORUS
Help is there, Queen, in all this woman says,
To ease thy suffering. But 'tis thee I praise;
Albeit that praise is harder to thine ear
Than all her chiding was, and bitterer!

PHAEDRA
Oh, this it is hath flung to dogs and birds
Men's lives and homes and cities-fair false word!
Oh, why speak things to please our ears? We crave
Not that. Tis honour, honour, we must save!

NURSE
Why prate so proud! 'Tis no words, brave nor base
Thou cravest; 'tis a man's arms!

[**PHAEDRA** moves indignantly.

Up and face
The truth of what thou art, and name it straight!
Were not thy life thrown open here for Fate
To beat on; hadst thou been a woman pure
Or wise or strong; never had I for lure
Of joy nor heartache led thee on to this!
But when a whole life one great battle is,
To win or lose—no man can blame me then.

PHAEDRA
Shame on thee! Lock those lips, and ne'er again
Let word nor thought so foul have harbour there!

NURSE

Foul, if thou wilt: but better than the fair
For thee and me. And better, too, the deed
Behind them, if it save thee in thy need,
Than that word Honour thou wilt die to win!

PHAEDRA

Nay, in God's name,—such wisdom and such sin
Are all about thy lips!—urge me no more.
For all the soul within me is wrought o'er
By Love; and if thou speak and speak, I may
Be spent, and drift where now I shrink away.

NURSE

Well, if thou wilt!—'Twere best never to err,
But, having erred, to take a counsellor
Is second.—Mark me now. I have within
love-philtres, to make peace where storm hath been,
That, with no shame, no scathe of mind, shall save
Thy life from anguish; wilt but thou be brave!

[To herself, rejecting.

Ah, but from him, the well-beloved, some sign
We need, or word, or raiment's hem, to twine
Amid the charm, and one spell knit from twain.

PHAEDRA

Is it a potion or a salve? Be plain.

NURSE

Who knows? Seek to be helped, Child, not to know.

PHAEDRA

Why art thou ever subtle? I dread thee, so.

NURSE

Thou wouldst dread everything!—What dost thou dread?

PHAEDRA

Least to his ear some word be whispered.

NURSE

Let be, Child! I will make all well with thee!
—Only do thou, O Cyprian of the Sea,
Be with me! And mine own heart, come what may,
Shall know what ear to seek, what word to say!

[The **NURSE**, having spoken these last words in prayer apart to the Statue of **CYPRIS**, turns back and goes into the house. **PHAEDRA** sits pensive again on her couch till towards the end of the following Song, when she rises and bends close to the door.

CHORUS
Erôs, Erôs, who blindest, tear by tear,
Men's eyes with hunger; thou swift Foe that pliest
Deep in our hearts joy like an edgèd spear;
Come not to me with Evil haunting near,
Wrath on the wind, nor jarring of the clear
Wing's music as thou fliest!
There is no shaft that burneth, not in fire,
Not in wild stars, far off and flinging fear,
As in thine hands the shaft of All Desire,
Erôs, Child of the Highest!

In vain, in vain, by old Alpheüs' shore
The blood of many bulls doth stain the river
And all Greece bows on Phoebus' Pythian floor;
Yet bring we to the Master of Man no store
The Keybearer, who standeth at the door
Close-barred, where hideth ever
The heart of the shrine. Yea, though he sack man's life
Like a sacked city, and moveth evermore
Girt with calamity and strange ways of strife,
Him have we worshipped never!

There roamed a Steed in Oechalia's wild,
A Maid without yoke, without Master,
And Love she knew not, that far King's child;
But he came, he came, with a song in the night.
With fire, with blood; and she strove in flight,
A Torrent Spirit, a Maenad white,
Faster and vainly faster,
Sealed unto Heracles by the Cyprian's Might.
Alas, thou Bride of Disaster!

O Mouth of Dirce, O god-built wall,
That Dirce's wells run under,
Ye know the Cyprian's fleet footfall!
Ye saw the heavens around her flare,
When she lulled to her sleep that Mother fair
Of twy-born Bacchus, and decked her there
The Bride of the bladed Thunder.
For her breath is on all that hath life, and she floats in the air,
Bee-like, death-like, a wonder.

[During the last lines **PHAEDRA** has approached the door and is listening.

PHAEDRA
Silence ye Women! Something is amiss.

LEADER
How? In the house?—Phaedra, what fear is this?

PHAEDRA
Let me but listen! There are voices. Hark!

LEADER
I hold my peace: yet is thy presage dark.

PHAEDRA
Oh, misery!
O God, that such a thing should fall on me!

LEADER
What sound, what word,
O Women, Friend, makes that sharp terror start
Out at thy lips? What ominous cry half-heard
Hath leapt upon thine heart?

PHAEDRA
I am undone!—Bend to the door and hark,
Hark what a tone sounds there, and sinks away!

LEADER
Thou art beside the bars. 'Tis thine to mark
The castle's floating message. Say, Oh, say
What thing hath come to thee?

PHAEDRA [Calmly]
Why, what thing should it be?
The son of that proud Amazon speaks again
In bitter wrath: speaks to my handmaiden!

LEADER
I hear a noise of voices, nothing clear.
For thee the din hath words, as through barred locks
Floating, at thy heart it knocks.

PHAEDRA
"Pander of Sin" it says.—Now canst thou hear?—
And there: "Betrayer of a master's bed."

LEADER
Ah me, betrayed! Betrayed!
Sweet Princess, thou art ill bested,
Thy secret brought to light, and ruin near,
By her thou heldest dear,
By her that should have loved thee and obeyed!

PHAEDRA

Aye, I am slain. She thought to help my fall
With love instead of honour, and wrecked all.

LEADER
Where wilt thou turn thee, where?
And what help seek, O wounded to despair?

PHAEDRA
I know not, save one thing to die right soon.
For such as me God keeps no other boon.

[The door in the centre bursts open, and **HIPPOLYTUS** comes forth, closely followed by the **NURSE**.
PHAEDRA cowers aside.

HIPPOLYTUS
O Mother Earth, O Sun that makest clean,
What poison have I heard, what speechless sin!

NURSE
Hush O my Prince, lest others mark, and guess ...

HIPPOLYTUS
I have heard horrors! Shall I hold my peace?

NURSE
Yea by this fair right arm, Son, by thy pledge ...

HIPPOLYTUS
Down with that hand! Touch not my garment's edge!

NURSE
Oh, by thy knees, be silent or I die!

HIPPOLYTUS
Why, when thy speech was all so guiltless? Why?

NURSE
It is not meet, fair Son, for every ear!

HIPPOLYTUS
Good words can bravely forth, and have no fear.

NURSE
Thine oath, thine oath! I took thine oath before!

HIPPOLYTUS
'Twas but my tongue, 'twas not my soul that swore.

NURSE
O Son, what wilt thou? Wilt thou slay thy kin?

HIPPOLYTUS

I own no kindred with the spawn of sin!

[He flings her from him.

NURSE

Nay, spare me! Man was born to err; oh, spare!

HIPPOLYTUS

O God, why hast Thou made this gleaming snare,
Woman, to dog us on the happy earth?
Was it Thy will to make Man, why his birth
Through Love and Woman? Could we not have rolled
Our store of prayer and offering, royal gold
Silver and weight of bronze before Thy feet,
And bought of God new child souls, as were meet
For each man's sacrifice, and dwelt in homes
Free, where nor Love nor Woman goes and comes
How, is that daughter not a bane confessed,
Whom her own sire sends forth—(He knows her best!)—
And, will some man but take her, pays a dower!
And he, poor fool, takes home the poison-flower;
Laughs to hang jewels on the deadly thing
He joys in; labours for her robe-wearing,
Till wealth and peace are dead. He smarts the less
In whose high seat is set a Nothingness,
A woman naught availing. Worst of all
The wise deep-thoughted! Never in my hall
May she sit throned who thinks and waits and sighs!
For Cypris breeds most evil in the wise,
And least in her whose heart has naught within;
For puny wit can work but puny sin.

Why do we let their handmaids pass the gate?
Wild beasts were best, voiceless and fanged, to wait
About their rooms, that they might speak with none,
Nor ever hear one answering human tone!
But now dark women in still chambers lay
Plans that creep out into light of day
On handmaids' lips—

[Turning to the **NURSE**.

As thine accursèd head
Braved the high honour of my Father's bed.
And came to traffic ... Our white torrent's spray
Shall drench mine ears to wash those words away!
And couldst thou dream that I ...? I feel impure
Still at the very hearing! Know for sure,
Woman, naught but mine honour saves ye both.
Hadst thou not trapped me with that guileful oath,

No power had held me secret till the King
Knew all! But now, while he is journeying,
I too will go my ways and make no sound.
And when he comes again, I shall be found
Beside him, silent, watching with what grace
Thou and thy mistress shall greet him face to face!
Then shall I have the taste of it, and know
What woman's guile is.—Woe upon you, woe!
How can I too much hate you, while the ill
Ye work upon the world grows deadlier still?
Too much? Make woman pure, and wild Love tame,
Or let me cry for ever on their shame!

[He goes off in fury to the left. **PHAEDRA** still cowering in her place begins to sob.

PHAEDRA
Sad, sad and evil-starred is Woman's state.
What shelter now is left or guard?
What spell to loose the iron knot of fate?
And this thing, O my God,
O thou sweet Sunlight, is but my desert!
I cannot fly before the avenging rod
Falls, cannot hide my hurt.
What help, O ye who love me, can come near,
What god or man appear,
To aid a thing so evil and so lost?
Lost, for this anguish presses, soon or late,
To that swift river that no life hath crossed.
No woman ever lived so desolate!

LEADER OF THE CHORUS
Ah me, the time for deeds is gone; the boast
Proved vain that spake thine handmaid; and all lost!

[At these words **PHAEDRA** suddenly remembers the **NURSE**, who is cowering silently where
HIPPOLYTUS had thrown her from him. She turns upon her.

PHAEDRA
O wicked, wicked, wicked! Murderess heart
To them that loved thee! Hast thou played thy part?
Am I enough trod down?

May Zeus, my sire,
Blast and uproot thee! Stab thee dead with fire!
Said I not—Knew I not thine heart?—to name
To no one soul this that is now my shame?
And thou couldst not be silent! So no more
I die in honour. But enough; a store
Of new words must be spoke and new things thought.
This man's whole being to one blade is wrought
Of rage against me. Even now he speeds

To abase me to the King with thy misdeeds;
Tell Pittheus; fill the land with talk of sin!

Cursèd be thou, and whoso else leaps in
To bring bad aid to friends that want it not.

[The **NURSE** has raised herself, and faces **PHAEDRA**, downcast but calm.

NURSE
Mistress, thou blamest me; and all thy lot
So bitter sore is, and the sting so wild,
I bear with all. Yet, if I would, my Child,
I have mine answer, couldst thou hearken aught.
I nursed thee, and I love thee; and I sought
Only some balm to heal thy deep despair,
And found—not what I sought for. Else I were
Wise, and thy friend, and good, had all sped right.
So fares it with us all in the world's sight.

PHAEDRA
First stab me to the heart, then humour me
With words! 'Tis fair; 'tis all as it should be!

NURSE
We talk too long, Child. I did ill; but, oh,
There is a way to save thee, even so!

PHAEDRA
A way? No more ways! One way hast thou trod
Already, foul and false and loathed of god!
Begone out of my sight; and ponder how
Thine own life stands! I need no helpers now.

[She turns from the **NURSE**, who creeps abashed away into the Castle.

Only do ye, high Daughters of Trozên,
Let all ye hear be as it had not been;
Know naught, and speak of naught! 'Tis my last prayer.

LEADER
By God's pure daughter, Artemis, I swear,
No word will I of these thy griefs reveal!

PHAEDRA
'Tis well. But now, yea, even while I reel
And falter, one poor hope, as hope now is,
I clutch at in this coil of miseries;
To save some honour for my children's sake;
Yea, for myself some fragment, though things break
In ruin around me. Nay, I will not shame
The old proud Cretan castle whence I came,

I will not cower before King Theseus' eyes,
Abased, for want of one life's sacrifice!

LEADER
What wilt thou? Some dire deed beyond recall?

PHAEDRA [Musing]
Die; but how die?

LEADER
Let not such wild words fall!

PHAEDRA [Turning upon her]
Give thou not such light counsel! Let me be
To sate the Cyprian that is murdering me!
To-day shall be her day; and, all strife past
Her bitter Love shall quell me at the last.
Yet, dying, shall I die another's bane!
He shall not stand so proud where I have lain
Bent in the dust! Oh, he shall stoop to share
The life I live in, and learn mercy there!

[She goes off wildly into the Castle.

CHORUS
Could I take me to some cavern for mine hiding,
In the hill-tops where the Sun scarce hath trod;
Or a cloud make the home of mine abiding,
As a bird among the bird-droves of God!
Could I wing me to my rest amid the roar
Of the deep Adriatic on the shore,
Where the waters of Eridanus are clear,
And Phaëthon's sad sisters by his grave
Weep into the river, and each tear
Gleams, a drop of amber, in the wave.

To the strand of the Daughters of the Sunset,
The Apple-tree, the singing and the gold;
Where the mariner must stay him from his onset,
And the red wave is tranquil as of old;
Yea, beyond that Pillar of the End
That Atlas guardeth, would I wend;
Where a voice of living waters never ceaseth
In God's quiet garden by the sea,
And Earth, the ancient life-giver, increaseth
Joy among the meadows, like a tree.

O shallop of Crete, whose milk-white wing
Through the swell and the storm-beating,
Bore us thy Prince's daughter,
Was it well she came from a joyous home

To a far King's bridal across the foam?
What joy hath her bridal brought her?
Sure some spell upon either hand
Flew with thee from the Cretan strand,
Seeking Athena's tower divine;
And there, where Munychus fronts the brine,
Crept by the shore-flung cables' line,
The curse from the Cretan water!

And for that dark spell that about her clings,
Sick desires of forbidden things
The soul of her rend and sever;
The bitter tide of calamity
Hath risen above her lips; and she,
Where bends she her last endeavour?
She will hie her alone to her bridal room,
And a rope swing slow in the rafters' gloom;
And a fair white neck shall creep to the noose,
A-shudder with dread, yet firm to choose
The one strait way for fame, and lose
The Love and the pain for ever.

[The Voice of the **NURSE** is heard from within, crying, at first inarticulately, then clearly.

VOICE
Help ho! The Queen! Help, whoso hearkeneth!
Help! Theseus' spouse caught in a noose of death!

A WOMAN
God, is it so soon finished? That bright head
Swinging beneath the rafters! Phaedra dead!

VOICE
O haste! This knot about her throat is made
So fast! Will no one bring me a swift blade?

A WOMAN
Say, friends, what think ye? Should we haste within,
And from her own hand's knotting loose the Queen?

ANOTHER
Nay, are there not men there? 'Tis an ill road
In life, to finger at another's load.

VOICE
Let it lie straight! Alas! the cold white thing
That guards his empty castle for the King!

A WOMAN
Ah! "Let it lie straight!" Heard ye what she said?
No need for helpers now; the Queen is dead!

[The **WOMEN**, intent upon the voices from the Castle, have not noticed the approach of **THESEUS**. He enters from the left; his dress and the garland on his head show that he has returned from some oracle or special abode of a God. He stands for a moment perplexed.

THESEUS
Ho, Women, and what means this loud acclaim
Within the house? The vassals' outcry came
To smite mine ears far off. It were more meet
To fling out wide the Castle gates, and greet
With a joy held from God's Presence!

[The confusion and horror of the **WOMEN'S FACES** gradually affects him. A dirge-cry comes from the Castle.

How?
Not Pittheus? Hath Time struck that hoary brow?
Old is he, old, I know. But sore it were,
Returning thus, to find his empty chair!

[The **WOMEN** hesitate; then the Leader comes forward.

LEADER
O Theseus, not on any old man's head
This stroke falls. Young and tender is the dead.

THESEUS
Ye Gods! One of my children torn from me?

LEADER
Thy motherless children live, most grievously.

THESEUS
How sayst thou? What? My wife? ...
Say how she died.
LEADER
In a high death-knot that her own hands tied.

THESEUS
A fit of the old cold anguish? Tell me all—
That held her? Or did some fresh thing befall?

LEADER
We know no more. But now arrived we be,
Theseus, to mourn for thy calamity.

[**THESEUS** stays for a moment silent, and puts his hand on his brow. He notices the wreath.

THESEUS
What? And all garlanded I come to her
With flowers, most evil-starred God's-messenger!

Ho, varlets, loose the portal bars; undo
The bolts; and let me see the bitter view
Of her whose death hath brought me to mine own.

[The great central door of the Castle is thrown open wide, and the body of **PHAEDRA** is seen lying on a bier, surrounded by a group of **HANDMAIDS**, wailing.

THE HANDMAIDS
Ah me, what thou hast suffered and hast done:
A deed to wrap this roof in flame!
Why was thine hand so strong, thine heart so bold?
Wherefore. O dead in anger, dead in shame,
The long, long wrestling ere thy breath was cold?
O ill-starred Wife,
What brought this blackness over all thy life?

[A throng of **MEN** and **WOMEN** has gradually collected.]

THESEUS
Ah me, this is the last
—Hear, O my countrymen!—and bitterest
Of Theseus' labours! Fortune all unblest,
How hath thine heavy heel across me passed!
Is it the stain of sins done long ago,
Some fell God still remembereth,
That must so dim and fret my life with death?
I cannot win to shore; and the waves flow
Above mine eyes, to be surmounted not.
Ah wife, sweet wife, what name
Can fit thine heavy lot?
Gone like a wild bird, like a blowing flame,
In one swift gust, where all things are forgot!
Alas! this misery!
Sure 'tis some stroke of God's great anger rolled
From age to age on me,
For some dire sin wrought by dim kings of old.

LEADER
Sire, this great grief hath come to many an one,
A true wife lost. Thou art not all alone.

THESEUS
Deep, deep beneath the Earth,
Dark may my dwelling be,
And night my heart's one comrade, in the dearth,
O Love, of thy most sweet society.
This is my death, O Phaedra, more than thine.

[He turns suddenly on the **ATTENDANTS**.

Speak who speak can! What was it? What malign

Swift stroke, O heart discounselled, leapt on thee?

[He bends over **PHAEDRA**; then, as no one speaks looks fiercely up.

What, will ye speak? Or are they dumb as death,
This herd of thralls, my high house harboureth?

[There is no answer. He bends again over **PHAEDRA**.

SOME WOMEN
Woe, woe! God brings to birth
A new grief here, close on the other's tread!
My life hath lost its worth.
May all go now with what is finishèd!
The castle of my King is overthrown,
A house no more, a house vanished and gone!

OTHER WOMEN
O God, if it may be in any way,
Let not this house be wrecked! Help us who pray!
I know not what is here: some unseen thing
That shows the Bird of Evil on the wing.

[**THESEUS** has read the tablet and breaks out in uncontrollable emotion.

THESEUS
Oh, horror piled on horror!—Here is writ...
Nay, who could bear it, who could speak of it?

LEADER
What, O my King? If I may hear it, speak!

THESEUS
Doth not the tablet cry aloud, yea, shriek,
Things not to be forgotten?—Oh, to fly
And hide mine head! No more a man am I.
God what ghastly music echoes here!

LEADER
How wild thy voice! Some terrible thing is near.

THESEUS
No; my lips' gates will hold it back no more;
This deadly word,
That struggles on the brink and will not o'er,
Yet will not stay unheard.

[He raises his hand, to make proclamation to all present.

Ho, hearken all this land!

[The **PEOPLE** gather expectantly about him.

Hippolytus by violence hath laid hand
On this my wife, forgetting God's great eye.

[Murmurs of amazement and horror; **THESEUS**, apparently calm, raises both arms to heaven.

Therefore, O Thou my Father, hear my cry,
Poseidon! Thou didst grant me for mine own
Three prayers; for one of these, slay now my son,
Hippolytus; let him not outlive this day,
If true thy promise was! Lo, thus I pray.

LEADER
Oh, call that wild prayer back! O King, take heed!
I know that thou wilt live to rue this deed.

THESEUS
It may not be.—And more, I cast him out
From all my realms. He shall be held about
By two great dooms. Or by Poseidon's breath
He shall fall swiftly to the house of Death;
Or wandering, outcast, o'er strange land and sea,
Shall live and drain the cup of misery.

LEADER
Ah; see! here comes he at the point of need.
Shake off that evil mood, O King; have heed
For all thine house and folk—Great Theseus, hear!

[**THESEUS** stands silent in fierce gloom. **HIPPOLYTUS** comes in from the right.

HIPPOLYTUS
Father, I heard thy cry, and sped in fear
To help thee, but I see not yet the cause
That racked thee so. Say, Father, what it was.

[The murmurs in the crowd, the silent gloom of his **FATHER**, and the horror of the **CHORUS-WOMEN**
gradually work on **HIPPOLYTUS** and bewilder him. He catches sight of the bier.

Ah, what is that! Nay, Father, not the Queen
Dead!

[Murmurs in the **CROWD**.

'Tis most strange. 'Tis passing strange, I ween.
'Twas here I left her. Scarce an hour hath run
Since here she stood and looked on this same sun.
What is it with her? Wherefore did she die?

[**THESEUS** remains silent. The murmurs increase.

Father, to thee I speak. Oh, tell me, why,
Why art thou silent? What doth silence know
Of skill to stem the bitter flood of woe?
And human hearts in sorrow crave the more,
For knowledge, though the knowledge grieve them sore.
It is not love, to veil thy sorrows in
From one most near to thee, and more than kin.

THESEUS [To himself]
Fond race of men, so striving and so blind,
Ten thousand arts and wisdoms can ye find,
Desiring all and all imagining:
But ne'er have reached nor understood one thing,
To make a true heart there where no heart is!

HIPPOLYTUS
That were indeed beyond man's mysteries,
To make a false heart true against his will.
But why this subtle talk? It likes me ill,
Father; thy speech runs wild beneath this blow.

THESEUS [As before]
O would that God had given us here below
Some test of love, some sifting of the soul,
To tell the false and true! Or through the whole
Of men two voices ran, one true and right,
The other as chance willed it; that we might
Convict the liar by the true man's tone,
And not live duped forever, every one!

HIPPOLYTUS [Misunderstanding him; then guessing at something of the truth]
What? Hath some friend proved false?
Or in thine ear
Whispered some slander? Stand I tainted here,
Though utterly innocent?

[Murmurs from the **CROWD**.

Yea, dazed am I;
'Tis thy words daze me, falling all awry,
Away from reason, by fell fancies vexed!

THESEUS
O heart of man, what height wilt venture next?
What end comes to thy daring and thy crime?
For if with each man's life 'twill higher climb,
And every age break out in blood and lies
Beyond its fathers, must not God devise
Some new world far from ours, to hold therein
Such brood of all unfaithfulness and sin?

Look, all, upon this man, my son, his life
Sprung forth from mine! He hath defiled my wife;
And standeth here convicted by the dead,
A most black villain!

[**HIPPOLYTUS** falls back with a cry and covers his face with his robe.

Nay, hide not thine head!
Pollution, is it? Thee it will not stain.
Look up, and face thy Father's eyes again!
Thou friend of Gods, of all mankind elect;
Thou the pure heart, by thoughts of ill unflecked!
I care not for thy boasts. I am not mad,
To deem that Gods love best the base and bad.
Now is thy day! Now vaunt thee; thou so pure,
No flesh of life may pass thy lips! Now lure
Fools after thee; call Orpheus King and Lord;
Make ecstasies and wonders! Thumb thine hoard
Of ancient scrolls and ghostly mysteries—
Now thou art caught and known!

Shun men like these,
I charge ye all! With solemn words they chase
their prey, and in their hearts plot foul disgrace.
My wife is dead.—"Ha, so that saves thee now,"
That is what grips thee worst, thou caitiff, thou!
What oaths, what subtle words, shall stronger be
Than this dead hand, to clear the guilt from thee?

"She hated thee," thou sayest; "the bastard born
Is ever sore and bitter as a thorn
To the true brood."—A sorry bargainer
In the ills and goods of life thou makest her,
If all her best-beloved she cast away
To wreck blind hate on thee!—What, wilt thou say
"Through every woman's nature one blind strand
Of passion winds, that men scarce understand?"—
Are we so different? Know I not the fire
And perilous flood of a young man's desire,
Desperate as any woman, and as blind,
When Cypris stings? Save that the man behind
Has all men's strength to aid him. Nay, 'twas thou...

But what avail to wrangle with thee now,
When the dead speaks for all to understand,
A perfect witness!

Hie thee from this land
To exile with all speed. Come never more
To god-built Athens, not to the utmost shore
Of any realm where Theseus' arm is strong!

What? Shall I bow my head beneath this wrong,
And cower to thee? Not Isthmian Sinis so
Will bear men witness that I laid him low,
Nor Skiron's rocks, that share the salt sea's prey,
Grant that my hand hath weight vile things to slay!

LEADER
Alas! whom shall I call of mortal men
Happy? The highest are cast down again.

HIPPOLYTUS
Father, the hot strained fury of thy heart
Is terrible. Yet, albeit so swift thou art
Of speech, if all this matter were laid bare,
Speech were not then so swift; nay, nor so fair...

[Murmurs again in the **CROWD**.

I have no skill before a crowd to tell
My thoughts. 'Twere best with few, that know me well.—
Nay that is natural; tongues that sound but rude
In wise men's ears, speak to the multitude
With music.

None the less, since there is come
This stroke upon me, I must not be dumb,
But speak perforce... And there will I begin
Where thou beganst, as though to strip my sin
Naked, and I not speak a word!

Dost see
This sunlight and this earth? I swear to thee
There dwelleth not in these one man—deny
All that thou wilt!—more pure of sin than I.

Two things I know on earth: God's worship first;
Next to win friends about me, few, that thirst
To hold them clean of all unrighteousness.
Our rule doth curse the tempters, and no less
Who yieldeth to the tempters.—How, thou say'st,
"Dupes that I jest at?" Nay; I make a jest
Of no man. I am honest to the end,
Near or far off, with him I call my friend.
And most in that one thing, where now thy mesh
Would grip me, stainless quite! No woman's flesh
Hath e'er this body touched. Of all such deed
Naught wot I, save what things a man may read
In pictures or hear spoke; nor am I fain,
Being virgin-souled, to read or hear again.
My life of innocence moves thee not; so be it.
Show then what hath seduced me; let me see it.

Was that poor flesh so passing fair, beyond
All woman's loveliness?

Was I some fond
False plotter, that I schemed to win through her
Thy castle's heirdom? Fond indeed I were!
Nay, a stark madman! "But a crown," thou sayest,
"Usurped, is sweet." Nay, rather most unblest
To all wise-hearted; sweet to fools and them
Whose eyes are blinded by the diadem.
In contests of all valour fain would I
Lead Hellas; but in rank and majesty
Not lead, but be at ease, with good men near
To love me, free to work and not to fear.
That brings more joy than any crown or throne.

[He sees from the demeanor of **THESEUS** and of the **CROWD** that his words are not winning them,
but rather making them bitterer than before. It comes to his lips to speak the whole truth.

I have said my say; save one thing...one alone
O had I here some witness in my need,
As I was witness! Could she hear me plead,
Face me and face the sunlight; well I know,
Our deeds would search us out for thee, and show
Who lies!

But now, I swear—so hear me both,
The Earth beneath and Zeus who Guards the Oath—
I never touched this woman that was thine!
No words could win me to it, nor incline
My heart to dream it. May God strike me down,
Nameless and fameless, without home or town,
An outcast and a wanderer of the world;
May my dead bones rest never, but be hurled
From sea to land, from land to angry sea,
If evil is my heart and false to thee!

[He waits a moment; but sees that his **FATHER** is unmoved. The truth again comes to his lips.

If 'twas some fear that made her cast away
Her life ... I know not. More I must not say.
Right hath she done when in her was no right;
And Right I follow to mine own despite!

LEADER
It is enough! God's name is witness large,
And thy great oath, to assoil thee of this charge,

THESEUS
Is not the man a juggler and a mage,
Cool wits and one right oath—what more?—to assuage

Sin and the wrath of injured fatherhood!

HIPPOLYTUS
Am I so cool? Nay, Father, 'tis thy mood
That makes me marvel! By my faith, wert thou
The son, and I the sire; and deemed I now
In very truth thou hadst my wife assailed,
I had not exiled thee, nor stood and railed,
But lifted once mine arm, and struck thee dead!

THESEUS
Thou gentle judge! Thou shalt not so be sped
To simple death, nor by thine own decree.
Swift death is bliss to men in misery.
Far off, friendless forever, thou shalt drain
Amid strange cities the last dregs of pain!

HIPPOLYTUS
Wilt verily cast me now beyond thy pale,
Not wait for Time, the lifter of the veil?

THESEUS
Aye, if I could, past Pontus, and the red
Atlantic marge! So do I hate thine head.

HIPPOLYTUS
Wilt weigh nor oath nor faith nor prophet's word
To prove me? Drive me from thy sight unheard?

THESEUS
This tablet here, that needs no prophet's lot
To speak from, tells me all. I ponder not
Thy fowls that fly above us! Let them fly.

HIPPOLYTUS
O ye great Gods, wherefore unlock not I
My lips, ere yet ye have slain me utterly,
Ye whom I love most? No. It may not be!
The one heart that I need I ne'er should gain
To trust me. I should break mine oath in vain.

THESEUS
Death! but he chokes me with his saintly tone!—
Up, get thee from this land! Begone! Begone!

HIPPOLYTUS
Where shall I turn me? Think. To what friend's door
Betake me, banished on a charge so sore?

THESEUS
Whoso delights to welcome to his hall

Vile ravishers ... to guard his hearth withal!

HIPPOLYTUS
Thou seekst my heart, my tears? Aye, let it be
Thus! I am vile to all men, and to thee!

THESEUS
There was a time for tears and thought; the time
Ere thou didst up and gird thee to thy crime.

HIPPOLYTUS
Ye stones, will ye not speak? Ye castle walls!
Bear witness if I be so vile, so false!

THESEUS
Aye, fly to voiceless witnesses! Yet here
A dumb deed speaks against thee, and speaks clear!

HIPPOLYTUS
Alas!
Would I could stand and watch this thing, and see
My face, and weep for very pity of me!

THESEUS
Full of thyself, as ever! Not a thought
For them that gave thee birth; nay, they are naught!

HIPPOLYTUS
O my wronged Mother! O my birth of shame!
May none I love e'er bear a bastard's name!

THESEUS [In a sudden blaze of rage]
Up, thralls, and drag him from my presence! What,
'Tis but a foreign felon! Heard ye not?

[The thralls still hesitate in spite of his fury.

HIPPOLYTUS
They touch me at their peril! Thine own hand
Lift, if thou canst, to drive me from the land.

THESEUS
That will I straight, unless my will be done!

[**HIPPOLYTUS** comes close to him and kneels.

Nay! Not for thee my pity! Get thee gone!

[**HIPPOLYTUS** rises, makes a sign of submission, and slowly moves away. **THESEUS**, as soon as he sees him going, turns rapidly and enters the Castle. The door is closed again. **HIPPOLYTUS** has stopped for a moment before the Statue of **ARTEMIS**, and, as **THESEUS** departs, breaks out in prayer.

HIPPOLYTUS
So; it is done! O dark and miserable!
I see it all, but see not how to tell
The tale.—O thou belovèd, Leto's Maid,
Chase-comrade, fellow-rester in the glade,
Lo, I am driven with a caitiff's brand
Forth from great Athens! Fare ye well, O land
And city of old Erechtheus! Thou, Trozên,
What riches of glad youth mine eyes have seen
In thy broad plain! Farewell! This is the end;
The last word, the last look!

Come, every friend
And fellow of my youth that still may stay,
Give me god-speed and cheer me on my way.
Ne'er shall ye see a man more pure of spot
Than me, though mine own Father loves me not!

[**HIPPOLYTUS** goes away to the right, followed by many Huntsmen and other young men. The rest of the **CROWD** has by this time dispersed, except the **WOMEN OF THE CHORUS** and some **MEN OF THE CHORUS OF HUNTSMEN**.

CHORUS
MEN
Surely the thought of the Gods hath balm in it alway, to win me
Far from my griefs; and a thought, deep in the dark of my mind,
Clings to a great Understanding. Yet all the spirit within me
Faints, when I watch men's deeds matched with the guerdon they find.
For Good comes in Evil's traces,
And the Evil the Good replaces;
And Life, 'mid the changing faces,
Wandereth weak and blind.

WOMEN
What wilt thou grant me, O God? Lo, this is the prayer of my travail—
Some well-being; and chance not very bitter thereby;
Spirit uncrippled by pain; and a mind not deep to unravel
Truth unseen, nor yet dark with the brand of a lie.
With a veering mood to borrow
Its light from every morrow,
Fair friends and no deep sorrow,
Well could man live and die!

MEN
Yet my spirit is no more clean,
And the weft of my hope is torn,
For the deed of wrong that mine eyes have seen,
The lie and the rage and the scorn;

A Star among men, yea, a Star
That in Hellas was bright,
By a Father's wrath driven far
To the wilds and the night.
Oh, alas for the sands of the shore!
Alas for the brakes of the hill,
Where the wolves shall fear thee no more,
And thy cry to Dictynna is still!

WOMEN
No more in the yoke of thy car
Shall the colts of Enetia fleet;
Nor Limna's echoes quiver afar
To the clatter of galloping feet.
The sleepless music of old,
That leaped in the lyre,
Ceaseth now, and is cold,
In the halls of thy sire.
The bowers are discrowned and unladen
Where Artemis lay on the lea;
And the love-dream of many a maiden
Lost, in the losing of thee.

A MAIDEN
And I, even I,
For thy fall, O Friend,
Amid tears and tears,
Endure to the end
Of the empty years,
Of a life run dry.
In vain didst thou bear him,
Thou Mother forlorn!
Ye Gods that did snare him,
Lo, I cast in your faces
My hate and my scorn!
Ye love-linkèd Graces,
(Alas for the day!)
Was he naught, then, to you,
That ye cast him away,
The stainless and true,
From the old happy places?

LEADER
Look yonder! 'Tis the Prince's man, I ween
Speeding toward this gate, most dark of mien.

[A **HENCHMAN** enters in haste.

HENCHMAN
Ye women, whither shall I go to seek
King Theseus? Is he in this dwelling? Speak!

LEADER
Lo, where he cometh through the Castle gate!

[**THESEUS** comes out from the Castle.

HENCHMAN
O King, I bear thee tidings of dire weight
To thee, aye, and to every man, I ween,
From Athens to the marches of Trozên.

THESEUS
What? Some new stroke hath touched, unknown to me,
The sister cities of my sovranty?

HENCHMAN
Hippolytus is...Nay, not dead; but stark
Outstretched, a hairsbreadth this side of the dark.

THESEUS [As though unmoved]
How slain? Was there some other man, whose wife
He had like mine denied, that sought his life?

HENCHMAN
His own wild team destroyed him, and the dire
Curse of thy lips.
The boon of thy great Sire
Is granted thee, O King, and thy son slain.

THESEUS
Ye Gods! And thou, Poseidon! Not in vain
I called thee Father; thou hast heard my prayer!
How did he die? Speak on. How closed the snare
Of Heaven to slay the shamer of my blood?

HENCHMAN
'Twas by the bank of beating sea we stood,
We thralls, and decked the steeds, and combed each mane;
Weeping; for word had come that ne'er again
The foot of our Hippolytus should roam
This land, but waste in exile by thy doom.

So stood we till he came, and in his tone
No music now save sorrow's, like our own,
And in his train a concourse without end
Of many a chase-fellow and many a friend.
At last he brushed his sobs away, and spake:
"Why this fond loitering? I would not break
My Father's law—Ho, there! My coursers four
And chariot, quick! This land is mine no more."

Thereat, be sure, each man of us made speed.
Swifter than speech we brought them up, each steed
Well dight and shining, at our Prince's side.
He grasped the reins upon the rail: one stride
And there he stood, a perfect charioteer,
Each foot in its own station set. Then clear
His voice rose, and his arms to heaven were spread:
"O Zeus, if I be false, strike thou me dead!
But, dead or living, let my Father see
One day, how falsely he hath hated me!"

Even as he spake, he lifted up the goad
And smote; and the steeds sprang. And down the road
We henchmen followed, hard beside the rein,
Each hand, to speed him, toward the Argive plain
And Epidaurus.

So we made our way
Up toward the desert region, where the bay
Curls to a promontory near the verge
Of our Trozên, facing the southward surge
Of Saron's gulf. Just there an angry sound,
Slow-swelling, like God's thunder underground
Broke on us, and we trembled. And the steeds
Pricked their ears skyward, and threw back their heads.
And wonder came on all men, and affright,
Whence rose that awful voice. And swift our sight
Turned seaward, down the salt and roaring sand.

And there, above the horizon, seemed to stand
A wave unearthly, crested in the sky;
Till Skiron's Cape first vanished from mine eye,
Then sank the Isthmus hidden, then the rock
Of Epidaurus. Then it broke, one shock
And roar of gasping sea and spray flung far,
And shoreward swept, where stood the Prince's car.

Three lines of wave together raced, and, full
In the white crest of them, a wild Sea-Bull
Flung to the shore, a fell and marvellous Thing.
The whole land held his voice, and answering
Roared in each echo. And all we, gazing there,
Gazed seeing not; 'twas more than eyes could bear.

Then straight upon the team wild terror fell.
Howbeit, the Prince, cool-eyed and knowing well
Each changing mood a horse has, gripped the reins
Hard in both hands; then as an oarsman strains
Up from his bench, so strained he on the thong,
Back in the chariot swinging. But the young
Wild steeds bit hard the curb, and fled afar;

Nor rein nor guiding hand nor morticed car
Stayed them at all. For when he veered them round,
And aimed their flying feet to grassy ground,
In front uprose that Thing, and turned again
The four great coursers, terror-mad. But when
Their blind rage drove them toward the rocky places,
Silent and ever nearer to the traces,
It followed rockward, till one wheel-edge grazed.

The chariot tript and flew, and all was mazed
In turmoil. Up went wheel-box with a din,
Where the rock jagged, and nave and axle-pin.
And there—the long reins round him—there was he
Dragging, entangled irretrievably.
A dear head battering at the chariot side,
Sharp rocks, and rippled flesh, and a voice that cried:
"Stay, stay, O ye who fattened at my stalls,
Dash me not into nothing!—O thou false
Curse of my Father!—Help! Help, whoso can,
An innocent, innocent and stainless man!"

Many there were that laboured then, I wot,
To bear him succour, but could reach him not,
Till—who knows how?—at last the tangled rein
Unclasped him, and he fell, some little vein
Of life still pulsing in him.

All beside,
The steeds, the hornèd Horror of the Tide,
Had vanished—who knows where?—in that wild land.
O King, I am a bondsman of thine hand;
Yet love nor fear nor duty me shall win
To say thine innocent son hath died in sin.
All women born may hang themselves, for me,
And swing their dying words from every tree
On Ida! For I know that he was true!

LEADER
O God, so cometh new disaster, new
Despair! And no escape from what must be!

THESEUS
Hate of the man thus stricken lifted me
At first to joy at hearing of thy tale;
But now, some shame before the Gods, some pale
Pity for mine own blood, hath o'er me come.
I laugh not, neither weep, at this fell doom.

HENCHMAN
How then? Behoves it bear him here, or how
Best do thy pleasure?—Speak, Lord. Yet if thou

Wilt mark at all my word, thou wilt not be
Fierce-hearted to thy child in misery.

THESEUS
Aye, bring him hither. Let me see the face
Of him who durst deny my deep disgrace
And his own sin; yea, speak with him, and prove
His clear guilt by God's judgments from above.

[The **HENCHMAN** departs to fetch **HIPPOLYTUS**; **THESEUS** sits waiting in stern gloom, while the **CHORUS** sing. At the close of their song a **DIVINE FIGURE** is seen approaching on a cloud in the air and the voice of **ARTEMIS** speaks.

CHORUS
Thou comest to bend the pride
Of the hearts of God and man,
Cypris; and by thy side,
In earth-encircling span,
He of the changing plumes,
The Wing that the world illumes,
As over the leagues of land flies he,
Over the salt and sounding sea.

For mad is the heart of Love,
And gold the gleam of his wing;
And all to the spell thereof
Bend, when he makes his spring;
All life that is wild and young
In mountain and wave and stream,
All that of earth is sprung,
Or breathes in the red sunbeam;
Yea, and Mankind. O'er all a royal throne,
Cyprian, Cyprian, is thine alone!

A VOICE FROM THE CLOUD
O thou that rulest in Aegeus' Hall,
I charge thee, hearken!
Yea, it is I,
Artemis, Virgin of God most High.
Thou bitter King, art thou glad withal
For thy murdered son?
For thine ear bent low to a lying Queen,
For thine heart so swift amid things unseen?
Lo, all may see what end thou hast won!
Go, sink thine head in the waste abyss;
Or aloft to another world than this,
Birdwise with wings,
Fly far to thine hiding,
Far over this blood that clots and clings;
For in righteous men and in holy things
No rest is thine nor abiding!

[The cloud has become stationary in the air.

Hear, Theseus, all the story of thy grief!
Verily, I bring but anguish, not relief;
Yet, 'twas for this I came, to show how high
And clean was thy son's heart, that he may die
Honoured of men; aye, and to tell no less
The frenzy, or in some sort the nobleness,
Of thy dead wife. One Spirit there is, whom we
That know the joy of white virginity,
Most hate in heaven. She sent her fire to run
In Phaedra's veins, so that she loved thy son.
Yet strove she long with love, and in the stress
Fell not, till by her Nurse's craftiness
Betrayed, who stole, with oaths of secrecy,
To entreat thy son. And he, most righteously,
Nor did her will, nor, when thy railing scorn
Beat on him, broke the oath that he had sworn,
For God's sake. And thy Phaedra, panic-eyed,
Wrote a false writ, and slew thy son, and died,
Lying; but thou wast nimble to believe!

[**THESEUS**, at first bewildered, then dumfounded, now utters a deep groan.

It stings thee, Theseus?—Nay, hear on and grieve
Yet sorer. Wottest thou three prayers were thine
Of sure fulfilment, from thy Sire divine?
Hast thou no foes about thee, then, that one—
Thou vile King!—must be turned against thy son?
The deed was thine. Thy Sea-born Sire but heard
The call of prayer, and bowed him to his word.
But thou in his eyes and in mine art found
Evil, who wouldst not think, nor probe, nor sound
The deeps of prophet's lore, nor day by day
Leave Time to search; but swifter than man may,
Let loose the curse to slay thine innocent son!

THESEUS
O Goddess, let me die!

ARTEMIS
Nay; thou hast done
A heavy wrong; yet even beyond this ill
Abides for thee forgiveness. 'Twas the will
Of Cypris that these evil things should be,
Sating her wrath. And this immutably
Hath Zeus ordained in heaven: no God may thwart
A God's fixed will; we grieve but stand apart.
Else, but for fear of the Great Father's blame,
Never had I to such extreme of shame

Bowed me, be sure, as here to stand and see
Slain him I loved best of mortality!
Thy fault, O King, its ignorance sunders wide
From very wickedness; and she who died
By death the more disarmed thee, making dumb
The voice of question. And the storm has come
Most bitterly of all on thee! Yet I
Have mine own sorrow, too. When good men die,
There is no joy in heaven, albeit our ire
On child and house of the evil falls like fire.

[A throng is seen approaching; **HIPPOLYTUS** enters, supported by his **ATTENDANTS**.

CHORUS
Lo, it is he! The bright young head
Yet upright there!
Ah the torn flesh and the blood-stained hair;
Alas for the kindred's trouble!
It falls as fire from a God's hand sped,
Two deaths, and mourning double.

HIPPOLYTUS
Ah, pain, pain, pain!
O unrighteous curse!   O unrighteous sire!
No hope.—My head is stabbed with fire,
And a leaping spasm about my brain.
Stay, let me rest. I can no more.
O fell, fell steeds that my own hand fed,
Have ye maimed me and slain, that loved me of yore?
—Soft there, ye thralls!   No trembling hands
As ye lift me, now!—Who is that that stands
At the right?—Now firm, and with measured tread,
Lift one accursèd and stricken sore
By a father's sinning.

Thou, Zeus, dost see me? Yea, it is I;
The proud and pure, the server of God,
The white and shining in sanctity!
To a visible death, to an open sod,
I walk my ways;
And all the labour of saintly days
Lost, lost, without meaning!

Ah God, it crawls
This agony, over me!
Let be, ye thralls!
Come, Death, and cover me:
Come, O thou Healer blest!

But a little more,
And my soul is clear,

And the anguish o'er!
Oh, a spear, a spear!
To rend my soul to its rest!

Oh, strange, false Curse! Was there some blood-stained head,
Some father of my line, unpunishèd,
Whose guilt lived in his kin,
And passed, and slept, till after this long day
It lights... Oh, why on me? Me, far away
And innocent of sin?

O words that cannot save!
When will this breathing end in that last deep
Pain that is painlessness? 'Tis sleep I crave.
When wilt thou bring me sleep,
Thou dark and midnight magic of the grave!

ARTEMIS
Sore-stricken man, bethink thee in this stress,
Thou dost but die for thine own nobleness.

HIPPOLYTUS
Ah!
O breath of heavenly fragrance! Though my pain
Burns, I can feel thee and find rest again.
The Goddess Artemis is with me here.

ARTEMIS
With thee and loving thee, poor sufferer!

HIPPOLYTUS
Dost see me, Mistress, nearing my last sleep?

ARTEMIS
Aye, and would weep for thee, if Gods could weep.

HIPPOLYTUS
Who now shall hunt with thee or hold thy quiver?

ARTEMIS
He dies but my love cleaves to him for ever.

HIPPOLYTUS
Who guide thy chariot, keep thy shrine-flowers fresh?

ARTEMIS
The accursed Cyprian caught him in her mesh!

HIPPOLYTUS
The Cyprian? Now I see it!—Aye, 'twas she.

ARTEMIS
She missed her worship, loathed thy chastity!

HIPPOLYTUS
Three lives by her one hand! 'Tis all clear now.

ARTEMIS
Yea, three; thy father and his Queen and thou.

HIPPOLYTUS
My father; yea, he too is pitiable!

ARTEMIS
A plotting Goddess tripped him, and he fell.

HIPPOLYTUS
Father, where art thou? ... Oh, thou sufferest sore!

THESEUS
Even unto death, child. There is joy no more.

HIPPOLYTUS
I pity thee in this coil; aye, more than me.

THESEUS
Would I could lie there dead instead of thee!

HIPPOLYTUS
Oh, bitter bounty of Poseidon's love!

THESEUS
Would God my lips had never breathed thereof!

HIPPOLYTUS [Gently]
Nay, thine own rage had slain me then, some wise!

THESEUS
A lying spirit had made blind mine eyes!

HIPPOLYTUS
Ah me!
Would that a mortal's curse could reach to God!

ARTEMIS
Let be! For not, though deep beneath the sod
Thou liest, not unrequited nor unsung
Shall this fell stroke, from Cypris' rancour sprung,
Quell thee, mine own, the saintly and the true!

My hand shall win its vengeance through and through,
Piercing with flawless shaft what heart soe'er

Of all men living is most dear to Her.
Yea, and to thee, for this sore travail's sake,
Honours most high in Trozên will I make;
For yokeless maids before their bridal night
Shall shear for thee their tresses; and a rite
Of honouring tears be thine in ceaseless store;
And virgin's thoughts in music evermore
Turn toward thee, and praise thee in the Song
Of Phaedra's far-famed love and thy great wrong.

O seed of ancient Aegeus, bend thee now
And clasp thy son. Aye, hold and fear not thou!
Not knowingly hast thou slain him; and man's way,
When Gods send error, needs must fall astray.

And thou, Hippolytus, shrink not from the King,
Thy father. Thou wast born to bear this thing.
Farewell! I may not watch man's fleeting breath,
Nor strain mine eyes with the effluence of death.
And sure that Terror now is very near.

[The cloud slowly rises and floats away.

HIPPOLYTUS
Farewell, farewell, most Blessèd! Lift thee clear
Of soiling men! Thou wilt not grieve in heaven
For my long love! ...Father, thou art forgiven.
It was Her will. I am not wroth with thee...
I have obeyed Her all my days! ...

Ah me,
The dark is drawing down upon mine eyes;
It hath me! ... Father! ... Hold me! Help me rise!

THESEUS [Supporting him in his arms]
Ah, woe! How dost thou torture me, my son!

HIPPOLYTUS
I see the Great Gates opening. I am gone.

THESEUS
Gone? And my hand red-reeking from this thing!

HIPPOLYTUS
Nay, nay; thou art assoiled of manslaying.

THESEUS
Thou leav'st me clear of murder? Sayst thou so?

HIPPOLYTUS
Yea, by the Virgin of the Stainless Bow!

THESEUS
Dear Son! Ah, now I see thy nobleness!

HIPPOLYTUS
Pray that a true-born child may fill my place.

THESEUS
Ah me, thy righteous and god-fearing heart!

HIPPOLYTUS
Farewell;
A long farewell, dear Father, ere we part!

[**THESEUS** bends down and embraces him passionately.

THESEUS
Not yet!—O hope and bear while thou hast breath!

HIPPOLYTUS
Lo, I have borne my burden. This is death...
Quick, Father; lay the mantle on my face.

[**THESEUS** covers his face with a mantle and rises.

THESEUS
Ye bounds of Pallas and of Pelops' race,
What greatness have ye lost!
Woe, woe is me!
Thou Cyprian, long shall I remember thee!

CHORUS
On all this folk, both low and high,
A grief hath fallen beyond men's fears.
There cometh a throbbing of many tears,
A sound as of waters falling.
For when great men die,
A mighty name and a bitter cry
Rise up from a nation calling.

[They move into the Castle, carrying the body of **HIPPOLYTUS**.

Hippolytus by Euripides

Translated from the Greek by Theodore Alois Buckley

Index of Contents

The Persons
The Argument
Scene
HIPPOLYTUS

THE ARGUMENT

Theseus was the son of Othra and Neptune, and king of the Athenians; and having married Hippolyta, one of the Amazons, he begat Hippolytus, who excelled in beauty and chastity. When his wife died, he married, for his second wife, Phædra, a Cretan, daughter of Minos, king of Crete, and Pasiphaë. Theseus, in consequence of having slain Pallas, one of his kinsmen, goes into banishment, with his wife, to Trœzene, where it happened that Hippolytus was being brought up by Pittheus: but Phædra having seen the youth was desperately enamored, not that she was incontinent, but in order to fulfill the anger of Venus, who, having determined to destroy Hippolytus on account of his chastity, brought her plans to a conclusion. She, concealing her disease, at length was compelled to declare it to her nurse, who had promised to relieve her, and who, though against her inclination, carried her words to the youth. Phædra, having learned that he was exasperated, eluded the nurse, and hung herself. At which time Theseus having arrived, and wishing to take her down that was strangled, found a letter attached to her, throughout which she accused Hippolytus of a design on her virtue. And he, believing what was written, ordered Hippolytus to go into banishment, and put up a prayer to Neptune, in compliance with which the god destroyed Hippolytus. But Diana declared to Theseus every thing that had happened, and blamed not Phædra, but comforted him, bereaved of his child and wife, and promised to institute honors in the place to Hippolytus.

SCENE

Trœzene.

It was acted in the archonship of Ameinon, in the fourth year of the 87th Olympiad. Euripides first, Jophon second, Jon third. This Hippolytus is the second of that name, and is called ΣΤΕΦΑΝΙΑΣ: but it appears to have been written the latest, for what was unseemly and deserved blame is corrected in this play. The play is ranked among the first.

HIPPOLYTUS

VENUS

Great in the sight of mortals, and not without a name am I the Goddess Venus, and in heaven: and of as many as dwell within the ocean and the boundaries of Atlas, beholding the light of the sun, those indeed, who reverence my authority, I advance to honor; but overthrow as many as hold themselves high toward me. For this is in sooth a property inherent even in the race of the Gods, that "they rejoice when honored by men." But quickly will I show the truth of these words: for the son of Theseus, born of the Amazon, Hippolytus, pupil of the chaste Pittheus, alone of the inhabitants of this land of Trœzene, says that I am of deities the vilest, and rejects the bridal bed, and will have nothing to do with marriage. But Dian, the sister of Phœbus, daughter of Jove, he honors, esteeming her the greatest of deities. And through the green wood ever accompanying the virgin, with his swift dogs he clears the beasts from off the earth, having formed a fellowship greater than mortal ought. This indeed I grudge him not; for wherefore should I? but wherein he has erred toward me, I will avenge me on Hippolytus this very day: and having cleared most of the difficulties beforehand, I need not much labor. For Phædra, his father's noble wife, having seen him, (as he was going once from the house of Pittheus to the land of Pandion, in order to see and afterward be fully admitted to the hallowed mysteries,) was smitten in her heart with fierce love by my design. And even before she came to this land of Trœzene, at the very rock of Pallas that overlooks this land, she raised a temple to Venus, loving an absent love; and gave out afterward, that the Goddess was honored with her temple for Hippolytus's sake. But now since Theseus has left the land of Cecrops, in order to avoid the pollution of the murder of the sons of Pallas, and is sailing to this land with his wife, having submitted to a year's banishment from his people; there indeed groaning and stricken with the stings of love, the wretched woman perishes in secret; and not one of her domestics is conscious of her malady. But this love must by no means fall to the ground in this way: but I will open the matter to Theseus, and it shall become manifest. And him that is our enemy shall the father kill with imprecations, which Neptune, king of the ocean, granted as a privilege to Theseus, that he should make no prayer thrice to the God in vain. But Phædra dies, an illustrious woman indeed, yet still she must die; for I will not make her ills of that high consequence, that will hinder my enemies from giving me such full vengeance as may content me. But, as I see the son of Theseus coming, having left the toil of the chase, I will depart from this spot. But with him a numerous train of attendants following behind raise a clamor, praising the Goddess Dian with hymns, for he knows not that the gates of hell are opened, and that this day is the last he beholds.

HIPPOLYTUS, ATTENDANTS.

HIPPOLYTUS

Follow, follow, singing the heavenly Dian, daughter of Jove; Dian, under whose protection we are.

ATTENDANT

Holy, holy, most hallowed offspring of Jove, hail! hail! O Dian, daughter of Latona and of Jove, most beauteous by far of virgins, who, born of an illustrious sire, in the vast heaven dwellest in the palace of Jove, that mansion rich in gold.

HIPPOLYTUS

Hail, O most beauteous, most beauteous of virgins in Olympus, Dian! For thee, my mistress, bear I this wreathed garland from the pure mead, where neither does the shepherd think fit to feed his flocks, nor yet came iron there, but the bee ranges over the pure and vernal mead, and Reverence waters it with river dews. Whosoever has chastity, not that which is taught in schools, but that which is by nature, for this description of persons it is lawful thence to pluck, but for the evil it is not lawful. But, O my dear mistress, receive this wreath to bind your golden tresses from a pious hand. For to me alone of mortals is allowed this privilege. With thee I am both present, and exchange words with thee, hearing thy voice, but not seeing thy countenance. But may I finish the last turn of my course of life, even as I began.

ATTENDANT
O king, (for the Gods alone ought we to call Lords,) will you hear somewhat from me, who advise you well?

HIPPOLYTUS
Most certainly, or else I should not seem wise.

ATTENDANT
Knowest thou then the law, which is established among men?

HIPPOLYTUS
I know not; but what is the one, about which thou askest me?

ATTENDANT
To hate haughtiness, and that which is disagreeable to all.

HIPPOLYTUS
And rightly; for what haughty mortal is not odious?

ATTENDANT
And in the affable is there any charm?

HIPPOLYTUS
A very great one indeed, and gain with little toil.

ATTENDANT
Dost thou suppose that the same thing holds also among the Gods?

HIPPOLYTUS
Certainly, forasmuch as we mortals use the laws of the Gods.

ATTENDANT
How is it then that thou addressest not a venerable Goddess?

HIPPOLYTUS
Whom? but take heed that thy mouth err not.

ATTENDANT
Venus, who hath her station at thy gates.

HIPPOLYTUS
I, who am chaste, salute her at a distance.

ATTENDANT
Venerable is she, however, and of note among mortals.

HIPPOLYTUS
Different Gods and men are objects of regard to different persons.

ATTENDANT
May you be blest, having as much sense as you require.

HIPPOLYTUS
No one of the Gods, that is worshiped by night, delights me.

ATTENDANT
My son, we must conform to the honors of the Gods.

HIPPOLYTUS
Depart, my companions, and having entered the house, prepare the viands: delightful after the chase is the full table.—And I must rub down my horses, that having yoked them to the car, when I am satiated with the repast, I may give them their proper exercise. But to your Venus I bid a long farewell.

ATTENDANT
But we, for one must not imitate the young, having our thoughts such, as it becomes slaves to give utterance to, will adore thy image, O Venus, our mistress; but thou shouldest pardon, if any one having intense feelings of mind by reason of his youth, speak foolishly: seem not to hear these things, for Gods must needs be wiser than men.

CHORUS
There is a rock near the ocean, distilling water, which sends forth from its precipices a flowing fountain, wherein they dip their urns; where was a friend of mine wetting the purple vests in the dew of the stream, and she laid them down on the back of the warm sunny cliff: from hence first came to me the report concerning my mistress, that she, worn with the bed of sickness, keeps her person within the house, and that fine vests veil her auburn head. And I hear that she this day for the third keeps her body untouched by the fruit of Ceres, which she receives not into her ambrosial mouth, wishing in secret suffering to hasten to the unhappy goal of death. For heaven-possessed, O lady, or whether by Pan, or by Hecate, or by the venerable Corybantes, or by the mother who haunts the mountains, thou art raving. But thou art thus tormented on account of some fault committed against the Cretan huntress, profane because of unoffered sacred cakes. For she goes through the sea and beyond the land on the eddies of the watery brine. Or some one in the palace misguides thy noble husband, the chief of the Athenians, by secret concubinage in thy bed. Or some sailor who put from port at Crete, hath sailed to the harbor most friendly to mariners, bringing some message to the queen; and, confined to her couch, she is bound in soul by sorrow for its sufferings. But wretched helplessness is wont to dwell with the wayward constitution of women, both on account of their throes and their loss of reason. Once through my womb shot this thrill, but I invoked the heavenly Dian, who gives easy throes, who presides over the bow, and to me she came ever much to be blessed, as well as the other Gods. But lo! the old nurse is bringing her out of the palace before the gates; and the sad cloud upon her brows is increased. What it can possibly be, my soul desires to know, with what can be afflicted the person of the queen, of color so changed.

PHÆDRA, NURSE, CHORUS.

Alas! the evils of men, and their odious diseases! what shall I do for thee? and what not do? lo! here is the clear light for thee, here the air: and now is thy couch whereon thou liest sick removed from out of the house: for every word you spoke was to come hither; but soon you will be in a hurry to go to your chamber back again: for you are soon changed, and are pleased with nothing. Nor does what is present delight you, but what is not present you think more agreeable. It is a better thing to be sick, than to tend the sick: the one is a simple ill, but with the other is joined both pain of mind and toil of hands. But the whole life of men is full of grief, nor is there rest from toils. But whatever else there be more dear than life, darkness enveloping hides it in clouds. Hence we appear to dote on this present state, because it gleams on earth, through inexperience of another life, and the non-appearance of the things beneath the earth. But we are blindly carried away by fables.

PHÆDRA

Raise my body, place my head upright—I am faint in the joints of my limbs, my friends, lay hold of my fair-formed hands, O attendants—The dressing on my head is heavy for me to support—take it off, let flow my ringlets on my shoulders.

NURSE

Be of good courage, my child, and do not thus painfully shift the posture of your body. But you will bear your sickness more easily both with quiet, and with a noble temper, for it is necessary for mortals to suffer misery.

PHÆDRA

Alas! alas! would I could draw from the dewy fountain the drink of pure waters, and that under the alders, and in the leafy mead reclining I might rest!

NURSE

O my child, what sayest thou? Wilt thou not desist from uttering these things before the multitude, blurting forth a speech of madness?

PHÆDRA

Bear me to the mountain—I will go to the wood, and by the pine-trees, where tread the dogs the slayers of beasts, pursuing the dappled hinds—By the Gods I long to cheer on the hounds, and by the side of my auburn hair to hurl the Thessalian javelin bearing the lanced weapon in my hand.

NURSE

Wherefore in the name of heaven, my child, do you hanker after these things? wherefore have you any anxiety for hunting? and wherefore do you long for the fountain streams? for by the towers there is a perpetual flow of water, whence may be your draught.

PHÆDRA

O Dian, mistress of Limna near the sea, and of the exercises of the rattling steeds, would that I were on thy plains, breaking the Henetian colts.

NURSE

Wherefore again have you madly uttered this word? at one time having ascended the mountain you set forth with the desire of hunting; but now again you long for the colts on the wave-beaten sands. These things demand much skill in prophecy to find out, who it is of the Gods that torments thee, O lady, and strikes mad thy senses.

PHÆDRA

Wretch that I am, what then have I committed? whither have I wandered from my sound mind? I have gone mad; I have fallen by the evil influence of some God. Alas! alas! unhappy that I am— Nurse, cover my head again, for I am ashamed of the things I have spoken: cover me; a tear trickles down my eyes, and my sight is turned to my disgrace. For to be in one's right mind causes grief: but madness is an ill; yet it is better to perish, nothing knowing of one's ills.

NURSE

I cover thee—but when in sooth will death cover my body? Length of life teaches me many things. For it behooves mortals to form moderate friendships with each other, and not to the very marrow of the soul: and the affections of the mind should be dissoluble, and so that we can slacken them, or tighten. But that one soul should feel pangs for two, as I now grieve for her, is a heavy burden. The concerns of life carried to too great an extent, they say, bring rather destruction than delight, and are rather at enmity with health. Thus I praise what is in extreme less than the sentiment of "Nothing in excess;" and the wise will agree with me.

CHORUS

O aged woman, faithful nurse of the queen Phædra, we see indeed the wretched state of this lady, but it is not clear what her disease is: but we would wish to inquire and hear from you.

NURSE

I know not by my inquiries; for she is not willing to speak.

CHORUS

Nor what is the origin of these pangs?

NURSE

You come to the same result; for she is silent with regard to all these things.

CHORUS

How feeble she is, and wasted away as to her body!

NURSE

How could it be otherwise, seeing that she has abstained from food these three days?

CHORUS

From the violence of her calamity is it, or does she endeavor to die?

NURSE

To die; but she fasts to the dissolution of her life.

CHORUS

An extraordinary thing you have been telling me, if this conduct meets the approbation of her husband.

NURSE

He nothing knows, for she conceals this calamity, and denies that she is ill.

CHORUS

But does he not guess it, looking into her face?

NURSE

How should he? for he is out of this country.

CHORUS

But do you not urge it as a matter of necessity, when you endeavor to ascertain her disease and the wandering of her senses?

NURSE

I have tried every thing, and have made no further advances. I will not however abate even now from my zeal, so that you being present may bear witness with me, how I behave to my mistress when in calamity—Come, dear child, let us both forget our former conversations; and be both thou more mild, having smoothed that contracted brow, and altered the bent of your design; and I giving up that wherein I did not do right to follow thee, will have recourse to other better words. And if indeed you are ill with any of those maladies that are not to be mentioned, these women here can allay the disease: but if it may be related to men, tell it, that the thing may be mentioned to physicians.—Well! why art thou silent? It doth not behoove thee to be silent, my child, but either shouldst thou convict me, if aught I say amiss, or yield to words well spoken.—Say something—look hither—O wretch that I am! Ladies, in vain do we undergo these toils, while we are as far off from our purpose as before: for neither then was she softened by our words, nor now does she give heed to us. Still however know (now then be more obstinate than the sea) that, if thou shalt die, thou wilt betray thy children, who will have no share in their paternal mansion. I swear by the warlike queen the Amazon, who brought forth a lord over thy children, base-born yet of noble sentiments, thou knowest him well, Hippolytus.

PHÆDRA

Ah me!

NURSE

This touches thee.

PHÆDRA

You have destroyed me, nurse, and by the Gods I entreat thee henceforth to be silent with respect to this man.

NURSE

Do you see? you judge well indeed, but judging well you are not willing both to assist your children and to save your own life.

PHÆDRA

I love my children; but I am wintering in the storm of another misfortune.

NURSE

You have your hands, my child, pure from blood.

PHÆDRA

My hands are pure, but my mind has some pollution.

NURSE

What! from some calamity brought on you by any of your enemies?

PHÆDRA

A friend destroys me against my will, himself unwilling.

NURSE

Has Theseus sinned any sin against thee?

PHÆDRA

Would that I never be discovered to have injured him.

NURSE
What then this dreadful thing that impels thee to die?

PHÆDRA
Suffer me to err, for against thee I err not.

NURSE
Not willingly dost thou do so, but 'tis through thee that I shall perish.

PHÆDRA
What are you doing? you oppress me, hanging on me with your hand.

NURSE
And never will I let go these knees.

PHÆDRA
Ills to thyself wilt thou hear, O wretched woman, if thou shalt hear these ills.

NURSE
Still will I cling: for what greater evil can befall me than to lose thee?

PHÆDRA
You will be undone. The thing however brings honor to me.

NURSE
And dost thou then hide what is useful, when I beseech thee?

PHÆDRA
Yes, for from base things we devise things noble.

NURSE
Wilt not thou, then, appear more noble by telling it?

PHÆDRA
Depart, by the Gods, and let go my hand!

NURSE
No in sooth, since thou givest me not the boon that were right.

PHÆDRA
I will give it; for I have respect unto the reverence of thy hand.

NURSE
Now will I be silent: for hence is it yours to speak.

PHÆDRA
O wretched mother, what a love didst thou love!

NURSE

That which she had for the bull, my child, or what is this thou meanest?

PHÆDRA

Thou, too, O wretched sister, wife of Bacchus!

NURSE

Child, what ails thee? thou speakest ill against thy relations.

PHÆDRA

And I the third, how unhappily I perish!

NURSE

I am struck dumb with amazement. Whither will thy speech tend?

PHÆDRA

To that point, whence we have not now lately become unfortunate.

NURSE

I know not a whit further of the things I wish to hear.

PHÆDRA

Alas! would thou couldst speak the things which I must speak.

NURSE

I am no prophetess so as to know clearly things hidden.

PHÆDRA

What is that thing, which they do call men's loving!

NURSE

The same, my child, a most delightful thing, and painful withal.

PHÆDRA

One of the two feelings I must perceive.

NURSE

What say'st? Thou lovest, my child? What man!

PHÆDRA

Him whoever he is, that is born of the Amazon.

NURSE

Hippolytus dost thou say?

PHÆDRA

From thyself, not me, you hear—this name.

NURSE

Ah me! what wilt thou go on to say? my child, how hast thou destroyed me! Ladies, this is not to be borne; I will not endure to live, hateful is the day, hateful the light I behold. I will hurl myself down, I will rid me of this body: I will remove from life to death—farewell—I no longer am. For the chaste are in love with what is evil, not willingly indeed, yet still they love. Venus then is no deity, but if there be aught mightier than deity, that is she, who hath destroyed both this my mistress, and me, and the whole house.

CHORUS

Thou didst hear, O thou didst hear the queen lamenting her wretched sufferings that should not be heard. Dear lady, may I perish before I come to thy state of mind! Alas me! alas! alas! O hapless for these pangs! O the woes that attend on mortals! Thou art undone, thou hast disclosed thy evils to the light. What time is this that has eternally awaited thee? Some new misfortune will happen to the house. And no longer is it obscure where the fortune of Venus sets, O wretched Cretan daughter.

PHÆDRA

Women of Trœzene, who inhabit this extreme frontier of the land of Pelops. Often at other times in the long season of night have I thought in what manner the life of mortals is depraved. And to me they seem to do ill, not from the nature of their minds, for many have good thoughts, but thus must we view these things. What things are good we understand and know, but practice not; some from idleness, and others preferring some other pleasures to what is right: for there are many pleasures in life-long prates, and indolence, a pleasing ill, and shame; but there are two, the one indeed not base, but the other the weight that overthrows houses, but if the occasion on which each is used, were clear, the two things would not have the same letters. Knowing them as I did these things beforehand, by no drug did I think I should so far destroy these sentiments, as to fall into an opposite way of thinking. But I will also tell you the course of my determinations. After that love had wounded me, I considered how best I might endure it. I began therefore from this time to be silent, and to conceal this disease. For no confidence can be placed in the tongue, which knows to advise the thoughts of other men, but itself from itself has very many evils. But in the second place, I meditated to bear well my madness conquering it by my chastity. But in the third place, since by these means I was not able to subdue Venus, it appeared to me best to die: no one will gainsay this resolution. For may it be my lot, neither to be concealed where I do noble deeds, nor to have many witnesses, where I act basely. Besides this I knew I was a woman—a thing hated by all. O may she most miserably perish who first began to pollute the marriage-bed with other men! From noble families first arose this evil among women: for when base things appear right to those who are accounted good, surely they will appear so to the bad. I hate moreover those women who are chaste in their language indeed, but secretly have in them no good deeds of boldness: who, how, I pray, O Venus my revered mistress, look they on the faces of their husbands, nor dread the darkness that aided their deeds, and the ceilings of the house, lest they should some time or other utter a voice? For this bare idea kills me, friends, lest I should ever be discovered to have disgraced my husband, or my children, whom I brought forth; but free, happy in liberty of speech may they inhabit the city of illustrious Athens, in their mother glorious! For it enslaves a man, though he be valiant-hearted, when he is conscious of his mother's or his father's misdeeds. But this alone they say in endurance compeers with life, an honest and good mind, to whomsoever it belong. But Time, when it so chance, holding up the mirror as to a young virgin, shows forth the bad, among whom may I be never seen!

CHORUS

Alas! alas! In every way how fair is chastity, and how goodly a report has it among men!

NURSE

My mistress, just now indeed thy calamity coming upon me unawares, gave me a dreadful alarm. But now I perceive I was weak; and somehow or other among mortals second thoughts are the wisest. For thou hast not suffered any thing excessive nor extraordinary, but the anger of the

Goddess hath fallen upon thee. Thou lovest—what wonder this? with many mortals.—And then will you lose your life for love? There is then no advantage for those who love others, nor to those who may hereafter, if they must needs die. For Venus is a thing not to be borne, if she rush on vehement. Who comes quietly indeed on the person who yields; but whom she finds haughty and of lofty notions, him taking (how thinkest thou?) she chastises. But Venus goes through air, and is on the ocean wave; and all things from her have their birth. She it is that sows and gives forth love, from whence all we on earth are engendered. As many indeed as ken the writings of the ancients, or are themselves ever among the muses, they know indeed, how that Jove was formerly inflamed with the love of Semele; they know too, how that formerly the lovely bright Aurora bore away Cephalus up to the Gods, for love, but still they live in heaven, and fly not from the presence of the Gods: but they acquiesce yielding, I ween, to what has befallen them. And wilt thou not bear it? Thy father then ought to have begotten thee on stipulated terms, or else under the dominion of other Gods, unless thou wilt be content with these laws. How many, thinkest thou, are in full and complete possession of their senses, who, when they see their bridal bed diseased, seem not to see it! And how many fathers, thinkest thou, have aided their erring sons in matters of love, for this is a maxim among the wise part of mankind, "that things that show not fair should be concealed." Nor should men labor too exactly their conduct in life, for neither would they do well to employ much accuracy in the roof wherewith their houses are covered; but having fallen into fortune so deep as thou hast, how dost thou imagine thou canst swim out? But if thou hast more things good than bad, mortal as thou art, thou surely must be well off. But cease, my dear child, from these evil thoughts, cease too from being haughty, for nothing else save haughtiness is this, to wish to be superior to the Gods. But, as thou art in love, endure it; a God hath willed it so: and, being ill, by some good means or other try to get rid of thy illness. But there are charms and soothing spells: there will appear some medicine for this sickness. Else surely men would be slow indeed in discoveries, if we women should not find contrivances.

CHORUS
Phædra, she speaks indeed most useful advice in thy present state: but thee I praise. Yet is this praise less welcome than her words, and to thee more painful to hear.

PHÆDRA
This is it that destroys cities of men and families well governed—words too fair. For it is not at all requisite to speak words pleasant to the ear, but that whereby one may become of fair report.

NURSE
Why dost thou talk in this grand strain? thou needest not gay decorated words, but a man: as soon as possible must those be found, who will speak out the plain straightforward word concerning thee. For if thy life were not in calamities of such a cast, I never would have brought thee thus far for the sake of lust, and for thy pleasure: but now the great point is to save thy life; and this is not a thing deserving of blame.

PHÆDRA
O thou that hast spoken dreadful things, wilt thou not shut thy mouth? and wilt not cease from uttering again those words most vile?

NURSE
Vile they are, but better these for thee than fair; but better will the deed be (if at least it will save thee), than the name, in the which while thou boastest, thou wilt die.

PHÆDRA

Nay do not, I entreat thee by the Gods (for thou speakest well, but base are the things thou speakest go beyond this, since rightly have I surrendered my life to love; but if thou speak base things in fair phrase, I shall be consumed, being cast into that evil which I am now avoiding.

NURSE
If in truth this be thy opinion, thou oughtest not to err, but if thou hast erred, be persuaded by me, for this is the next best thing thou canst do. I have in the house soothing philters of love (and they but lately came into my thought); which, by no base deed, nor to the harm of thy senses, will rid you of this disease, unless you are obstinate. But it is requisite to receive from him that is the object of your love, some token, either some word, or some relic of his vest, and to join from two one love.

PHÆDRA
But is the charm an unguent or a potion?

NURSE
I know not: wish to be relieved, not informed, my child.

PHÆDRA
I fear thee, lest thou should appear too wise to me.

NURSE
Know that you would fear every thing, if you fear this, but what is it you are afraid of?

PHÆDRA
Lest you should tell any of these things to the son of Theseus.

NURSE
Let be, my child, I will arrange these matters honorably, only be thou my coadjutor, O Venus, my revered mistress; but the other things which I purpose, it will suffice to tell to my friends within.

CHORUS, PHÆDRA.

CHORUS
Love, love, O thou that instillest desire through the eyes, inspiring sweet affection in the souls of those against whom thou makest war, mayst thou never appear to me to my injury, nor come unmodulated: for neither is the blast of fire nor the bolt of heaven more vehement, than that of Venus, which Love, the boy of Jove, sends from his hands. In vain, in vain, both by the Alpheus, and at the Pythian temples of Phœbus does Greece then solemnize the slaughter of bulls: but Love, the tyrant of men, porter of the dearest chambers of Venus, we worship not, the destroyer and visitant of men in all shapes of calamity, when he comes. That virgin in Œchalia, yoked to no bridal bed, till then unwedded, and who knew no husband, having taken from her home a wanderer impelled by the oar, her, like some Bacchanal of Pluto, with blood, with smoke, and murderous hymeneals did Venus give to the son of Alcmena. O unhappy woman, because of her nuptials! O sacred wall of Thebes, O mouth of Dirce, you can assist me in telling, in what manner Venus comes: for by the forked lightning, by a cruel fate, did she put to eternal sleep the parent of the Jove-begotten Bacchus, when she was visited as a bride. For dreadful doth she breathe on all things, and like some bee hovers about.

PHÆDRA
Women, be silent: I am undone.

CHORUS

What is there that affrights thee, Phædra, in thine house?

PHÆDRA

Be silent, that I may make out the voice of those within.

CHORUS

I am silent: this however is an evil bodement.

PHÆDRA

Alas me! O! O! O! oh unhappy me, because of my sufferings!

CHORUS

What sound dost thou utter? what word speakest thou? tell me what report frightens thee, lady, rushing upon thy senses!

PHÆDRA

We are undone. Do you, standing at these gates, hear what the noise is that strikes on the house?

CHORUS

Thou art by the gate, the noise that is sent forth from the house is thy care. But tell me, tell me, what evil, I pray thee, came to thine ears?

PHÆDRA

The son of the warlike Amazon, Hippolytus, cries out, abusing in dreadful forms my attendant.

CHORUS

I hear indeed a noise, but can not plainly tell how it is. The voice came, it came through to the door.

PHÆDRA

But hark! he calls her plainly the pander of wickedness, the betrayer of her master's bed.

CHORUS

Alas me for thy miseries! Thou art betrayed, dear mistress. What shall I counsel thee? for hidden things are come to light, and thou art utterly destroyed—

PHÆDRA

O! O!

CHORUS

Betrayed by thy friends.

PHÆDRA

She hath destroyed me by speaking of my unhappy state, kindly but not honorably endeavoring to heal this disease.

CHORUS

How then? what wilt thou do, O thou that hast suffered things incurable?

PHÆDRA

I know not, save one thing; to die as soon as possible is the only cure of my present sufferings.

HIPPOLYTUS, PHÆDRA, NURSE, CHORUS.

HIPPOLYTUS
O mother earth, and ye disclosing rays of the sun, of what words have I heard the dreadful sound!

NURSE
Be silent, my son, before any one hears thy voice.

HIPPOLYTUS
It is not possible for me to be silent, when I have heard such dreadful things.

NURSE
Nay, I implore thee by thy beauteous hand.

HIPPOLYTUS
Wilt not desist from bringing thy hand near me, and from touching my garments?

NURSE
O! by thy knees, I implore thee, do not utterly destroy me.

HIPPOLYTUS
But wherefore this? since, thou sayest, thou hast spoken nothing evil.

NURSE
This word, my son, is by no means to be divulged.

HIPPOLYTUS
It is more fair to speak fair things to many.

NURSE
O my child, by no means dishonor your oath.

HIPPOLYTUS
My tongue hath sworn—my mind is still unsworn.

NURSE
O my son, what wilt thou do? wilt thou destroy thy friends?

HIPPOLYTUS
Friends! I reject the word: no unjust person is my friend.

NURSE
Pardon, my child: that men should err is but to be expected.

HIPPOLYTUS
O Jove, wherefore in the name of heaven didst thou place in the light of the sun that specious evil to men, women? for if thou didst will to propagate the race of mortals, there was no necessity for this to be done by women, but men might, having placed an equivalent in thy temples, either in brass, or iron, or the weighty gold, buy a race of children, each for the consideration of the value paid, and thus might dwell in unmolested houses, without females. But now, first of all, when we prepare to

bring this evil to our homes, we squander away the wealth of our houses. By this too it is evident, that woman is a great evil; for the father, who begat her and brought her up, having given her a dowry sends her away in order to be rid of the evil. But the husband, on the other hand, when he has received the baneful evil into his house, rejoices, having added a beautiful decoration to a most vile image, and tricks her out with robes, unhappy man, while he has been insensibly minishing the wealth of the family. But he is constrained; so that having made alliance with noble kinsmen, he retains with seeming joy a marriage bitter to him: or if he has received a good bride, but worthless parents in law, he suppresses the evil that has befallen him by the consideration of the good. But his state is the easiest, whose wife is settled in his house, a cipher, but useless by reason of simplicity. But a wise woman I detest: may there not be in my house at least a woman more highly gifted with mind than woman ought to be. For Venus engenders mischief rather among clever women, but a woman who is not endowed with capacity, by reason of her small understanding, is removed from folly. But it is right that an attendant should have no access to a woman, but with them ought to dwell the speechless brute beasts, in which case they would be able neither to address any one, nor from them to receive a voice in return. But now, they that are evil follow after their evil devices within, and the servants carry it forth abroad. As thou also hast, O evil woman, come to the purpose of admitting me to share a bed which must not be approached—a father's. Which impious things I will wash out with flowing stream, pouring it into my ears: how then could I be the vile one, who do not even deem myself pure, because I have heard such things?—But be well assured, my piety protects thee, woman, for, had I not been taken unawares by the oaths of the Gods, never would I have refrained from telling these things to my father. But now will I depart from the house, and stay during the time that Theseus is absent from the land, and will keep my mouth silent; but I will see, returning with my father's return, how you will look at him, both you and your mistress. But your boldness I shall know, having before had proof of it. May you perish: but never shall I take my fill of hating women, not even if any one assert, that I am always saying this. For in some way or other they surely are always bad. Either then let some one teach them to be modest, or else let him suffer me ever to utter my invectives against them.

CHORUS, PHÆDRA, NURSE.

CHORUS
Oh unhappy ill-fated fortune of women! what art now or what words have we, having failed as we have, to extricate the knot caused by these words?

PHÆDRA
We have met a just reward; O earth, and light, in what manner, I pray, can I escape from my fortunes? and how, my friends, can I conceal my calamity? Who of the Gods will appear my succorer, or what mortal my ally, or my fellow-worker in unjust works? for the suffering of my life that is at present on me comes hardly to be escaped. I am the most ill-fated of women.

CHORUS
Alas! alas! we are undone, lady, and the arts of thy attendant have not succeeded, and it fares ill with us.

PHÆDRA
O thou most vile, and the destruction of thy friends, what hast thou done to me! May Jove, my ancestor, tear thee up by the roots, having stricken thee by his fire. Did not I tell thee (did not I foresee thy intention?) to be silent with regard to those things with which I am now tormented? but thou couldst not refrain; wherefore I can no longer die with glory: but I must now in sooth employ new measures. For he, now that his mind is made keen with rage, will tell, to my detriment, thy errors to his father, and will fill the whole earth with the most vile reports. Mayst thou perish, both

thou and whoever else is forward to assist friends against their will otherwise than by honorable means.

NURSE
Lady, thou canst indeed blame the evil I have wrought; for that which gnaws upon thee masters thy better judgment;—but I too have somewhat to say in answer to these things, if thou wilt admit it: I brought thee up, and have a kind affection toward thee; but, while searching for medicine for thy disease, I found not that I wished for. But if I had succeeded, I had been surely ranked among the wise; for we have the reputation of sense according to our success.

PHÆDRA
What? is this conduct just, and satisfactory to me, to injure me first, and then to meet me in argument?

NURSE
We talk too long—I did not behave wisely. But even from this state of things it is possible that thou mayest be saved, my child.

PHÆDRA
Desist from speaking; for before also thou didst not well advise for me, and didst attempt evil things. But depart from my sight, and take care about thyself; for I will settle my own affairs in an honorable manner. But you, noble daughters of Trœzene, grant thus much to me requesting it, bury in silence what you here have heard.

CHORUS
I swear by hallowed Dian, daughter of Jove, that I will never reveal to the face of day one of thy evils.

PHÆDRA
Thou hast well spoken: but one kind of resource, while I search around me, do I find for my present calamity, so that I may make the life of my children glorious, and may myself be assisted as things have now fallen out. For never will I disgrace the house of Crete at least, nor will I come before the face of Theseus having acted basely, for one's life's sake.

CHORUS
But what irremediable evil art thou then about to perpetrate?

PHÆDRA
To die: but how, this will I devise.

CHORUS
Speak words of better omen.

PHÆDRA
And do thou at least advise me well. But having quitted life this day, I shall gratify Venus, who destroys me, and shall be conquered by bitter love. But when I am dead, I shall be an evil to another at least, so that he may know not to exult over my misfortunes; but, having shared this malady in common with me, he shall learn to be modest.

CHORUS
Would that I were under the rocks' vast retreats, and that there the God would make me a winged bird among the swift flocks, and that I were lifted up above the ocean wave that dashes against the

Adriatic shore, and the water of Eridanus, where for grief of Phaethon the thrice wretched virgins let fall into their father's billow the amber-beaming brightness of their tears: and that I could make my way to the shore where the apples grow of the harmonious daughters of Hesperus, where the ruler of the ocean no longer permits the passage of the purple sea to mariners, dwelling in that dread bourn of heaven which Atlas doth sustain, and the ambrosial founts stream forth hard by the couches of Jove's palaces, where the divine and life-bestowing earth increases the bliss of the Gods. O white-winged bark of Crete, who didst bear my queen through the perturbed ocean wave of brine from a happy home, thereby aiding her in a most evil marriage. For surely in both instances, or at any rate from Crete she came ill-omened to renowned Athens, when on the Munychian shore they bound the platted ends of their cables, and disembarked on the continent. Wherefore she was heartbroken with the terrible disease of unhallowed love by the influence of Venus; and now that she can no longer hold out against the heavy calamity, she will fit around her the noose suspended from the ceiling of her bridal chamber, adjusting it to her white neck, having revered the hateful Goddess, and embracing an honorable name, and ridding from her breast the painful love.

FEMALE SERVANT, CHORUS, THESEUS.

FEMALE SERVANT
Alack! alack! run to my succor all that are near the house—My mistress the wife of Theseus is hanging.

CHORUS
Alas! alas! the deed is done: the queen is indeed no more—she is suspended in the noose that hangs there.

FEMALE SERVANT
Will ye not haste? will not some one bring a two-edged sword, with which we may undo this knot around her neck?

SEMI-CHORUS
My friends, what do we? does it seem good to enter the house and to free the queen from the tight-drawn noose?

SEMI-CHORUS
Why we? Are not the young men-servants at hand? The being over-busy is not a safe plan through life.

FEMALE SERVANT
Lay right the wretched corpse, pull her limbs straight. A grievous housekeeping this for my master!

CHORUS
The unhappy woman, as I hear, has perished, for already are they laying her out as a corpse.

THESEUS
Know ye, females, what noise this is in my house? a heavy sound of my attendants reached me. For the family does not think fit to open the gates to me and to hail me with joy as having returned from the oracle. Has any ill befallen the aged Pittheus? His life is now indeed far advanced; but still he would be much lamented by us, were he to leave this house.

CHORUS

This that has happened, Theseus, extends not to the old; the young are they that by their death will grieve thee.

THESEUS
Alas me! is the life of any of my children stolen from me?

CHORUS
They live, but their mother is dead in a way that will grieve thee most.

THESEUS
What sayest? My wife dead? By what fate?

CHORUS
She suspended the noose, wherewith she strangled herself.

THESEUS
Wasted with sorrow, or from some sudden calamity?

CHORUS
Thus much we know—nothing further; for I am but just come to thy house, Theseus, to bewail thy evils.

THESEUS
Alas! alas! why then have I my head crowned with entwined leaves, who am the unhappy inquirer of the oracle? Servants, undo the bars of the gates; unloose the bolts, that I may behold the mournful spectacle of my wife, who by her death hath utterly undone me.

CHORUS
Alas! alas! unhappy for thy wretched ills: thou hast been a sufferer; thou hast perpetrated a deed of such extent as to throw this house into utter confusion. Alas! alas! thy boldness, O thou who hast died a violent death, and, by an unhallowed chance, the act committed by thy wretched hand. Who is it then, thou unhappy one, that destroys thy life?

THESEUS
Alas me for my sufferings! I have suffered, unhappy wretch, the extreme of my troubles—O fortune, how heavy hast thou come upon me and my house, an imperceptible spot from some evil demon! the wearing out of a life not to be endured; and I, unhappy wretch, perceive a sea of troubles so great, that never again can I emerge from it, nor escape beyond the flood of this calamity. What mention making can I unhappy, what heavy-fated fortune of thine, lady, saying that it was, can I be right? For as some bird thou art vanished from my hand, having leaped me a sudden leap to the realms of Pluto. Alas! alas! wretched, wretched are these sufferings, but from some distant period or other receive I this calamity from the Gods, for the errors of some of those of old.

CHORUS
Not to thee alone, O king, have these evils happened; but with many others thou hast lost an excellent wife.

THESEUS
In the shades beneath the earth, I unhappy wish, dying, to dwell in darkness, reft as I am of thy most dear company, for thou hast destroyed rather than perished—What then do I hear? whence came the deadly chance, lady, to thine heart? Will any speak what has happened, or does my royal palace

contain to no purpose the crowd of my attendants?—Alas me on thy account! unhappy that I am, what grief in my house have I seen, intolerable, indescribable! but—we are undone! my house left desolate, and my children orphans.

CHORUS
Thou hast left us, thou hast left us, O dear among women, and most excellent of those as many as both the light of the sun, and the star-visaged moon of night behold. O unhappy man! how great ill doth the house contain! with tears gushing over, my eyelids are wet at thy calamity. But the woe that will ensue on this I have long since been dreading.

THESEUS
Alas! alas! What I pray is this letter suspended from her dear hand? does it mean to betoken some new calamity?—What, has the unhappy woman written injunctions to me, making some request about my bridal bed and my children? Be of good courage, hapless one; for no woman exists, who shall enter the bed and the house of Theseus. But lo! the impressions of the golden seal of her no more here court my attention. Come, let me unfold the envelopments of the seal, and see what this letter should say to me.

CHORUS
Alas! alas! this new evil in succession again doth the God bring on. To me indeed the condition of life will be impossible to bear, from what has happened; for I consider, alas! as ruined and no more the house of my kings. O God, if it be in any way possible, do not overthrow the house; but hear me as I pray, for from some quarter, as though a prophet, I behold an evil omen.

THESEUS
Ah me! what other evil is this in addition to evil, not to be borne, nor spoken! alas wretched me!

CHORUS
What is the matter? Tell me if it may be told me.

THESEUS
It cries out—the letter cries out things most dreadful: which way can I fly the weight of my ills; for I perish utterly destroyed. What, what a complaint have I seen speaking in her writing!

CHORUS
Alas! thou utterest words foreboding woes.

THESEUS
No longer will I keep within the door of my lips this dreadful, dreadful evil hardly to be uttered. O city, city, Hippolytus has dared by force to approach my bed, having despised the awful eye of Jove. But O father Neptune, by one of these three curses, which thou formerly didst promise me, by one of those destroy my son, and let him not escape beyond this day, if thou hast given me curses that shall be verified.

CHORUS
O king, by the Gods recall back this prayer, for hereafter you will know that you have erred; be persuaded by me.

THESEUS
It can not be: and moreover I will drive him from this land. And by one or other of the two fates shall he be assailed: for either Neptune shall send him dead to the mansions of Pluto, having respect unto

my wish; or else banished from this country, wandering over a foreign land, he shall drag out a miserable existence.

CHORUS
And lo! thy son Hippolytus is present here opportunely, but if thou let go thy evil displeasure, king Theseus, thou wilt advise the best for thine house.

HIPPOLYTUS, THESEUS, CHORUS.

HIPPOLYTUS
I heard thy cry, my father, and came in haste; the thing however, for which you are groaning, I know not; but would fain hear from you. Ha! what is the matter? I behold thy wife, my father, a corpse: this is a thing meet for the greatest wonder.—Her, whom I lately left, her, who beheld the light no great time since. What ails her? In what manner died she, my father, I would fain hear from you. Art silent? But there is no use of silence in misfortunes; for the heart which desires to hear all things, is found eager also in the case of ills. It is not indeed right, my father, to conceal thy misfortunes from friends, and even more than friends.

THESEUS
O men, who vainly go astray in many things, why then do ye teach ten thousand arts, and contrive and invent every thing; but one thing ye do not know, nor yet have investigated, to teach those to be wise who have no intellect!

HIPPOLYTUS
A clever sophist this you speak of, who is able to compel those who have no wisdom to be rightly wise. But (for thou art arguing too refinedly on no suitable occasion) I fear, O father, lest thy tongue be talking at random through thy woes.

THESEUS
Alas! there ought to be established for men some infallible proof of their friends, and some means of knowing their dispositions, both who is true, and who is not a friend, and men ought all to have two voices, the one true, the other as it chanced, that the untrue one might be convicted by the true, and then we should not be deceived.

HIPPOLYTUS
Has some one then falsely accused me in your ear, and am I suffering who am not at all guilty? I am amazed, for your words, wandering beyond the bounds of reason, do amaze me.

THESEUS
Alas! the mind of man, to what lengths will it go? what will be the limit to its boldness and temerity? For if it shall increase with each generation of man, and the successor shall be wicked a degree beyond his predecessor, it will be necessary for the Gods to add to the earth another land, which will contain the unjust and the evil ones.—But look: ye on this man, who being born of me hath defiled my bed, and is manifestly convicted by the deceased of being most base.—But, since thou hast come to this attaint, show thy face here before thy father. Dost thou forsooth associate with the Gods, as being an extraordinary person? art thou chaste and uncontaminated with evil? I will not believe thy boasts, attributing (as I must, if I do believe) to the Gods the folly of thinking evil. Now then vaunt, and with thy feeding on inanimate food retail your doctrines upon men, and having Orpheus for your master, revel it, reverencing the emptiness of many letters; which avail you not; since you are caught.

But such sort of men I warn all to shun; for they hunt with fair-sounding words, while they devise base things. She is dead: dost thou think this will save thee? By this thou art most detected, O thou most vile one! For what sort of oaths, what arguments can be more strong than what she says, so that thou canst escape the accusation? Wilt thou say that she hated thee, and that the bastard race is hateful forsooth to those of noble birth? A bad housewife then of life you account her, if through hatred of thee she lost what was most dear to her. But wilt thou say that there is not this folly in men, but that there is in women? I myself have known young men who were not a whit more steady than women, when Venus disturbed the youthful mind: but their pretense of manliness protects them. Now however, why do I thus contend against thy words, when the corse, the surest witness, is here? Depart an exile from this land as soon as possible. And neither go to the divine-built Athens, nor to the confines of that land over which my sceptre rules. For if I thus suffering by thee be vanquished, never will the Isthmian Sinis bear witness of me that I killed him, but will say that I vainly boast. Nor will the Scironian rocks, that dwell by the sea, confess that I am formidable to the bad.

CHORUS
I know not how I can say that any of mortals is happy; for the things that were most excellent are turned back again.

HIPPOLYTUS
Father, thy rage indeed, and the commotion of thy mind is terrible; this thing, however, though it have fair arguments, if any one unravel it, is not fair. But I am unadorned with phrase to speak to the multitude, but to speak to my equals and to a few, more expert: but this also has consistency in it; for those, who are of no account among the wise, are more fitted to speak before the rabble. But yet it is necessary for me, since this calamity has come, to unloose my tongue. But first will I begin to speak from that point where first you attacked, as though you would destroy, and as though I should not answer again. Dost thou behold this light and this earth? In these there is not a man more chaste than me, not even though thou deny it. For, first indeed, I know to reverence the Gods, and to have such friends as attempt not to be unjust, but those, to whom there is modesty, so that neither they give utterance to evil thoughts, nor minister in return base services to those who use their friendship: nor am I the derider of my associates, O father, but the same man to my friends when they are not present, and when I am with them. But of one thing by which thou thinkest to crush me, I am pure; for to this day my body is undefiled by the couch of love; and I know not the deed except hearing of it by report, and seeing it in a picture, nor even am I forward to look at these things, having a virgin mind. And perhaps my modesty persuades you not. Behooves it thee then to show in what manner I lost it. Did this woman's person excel in beauty all women? Or did I hope to rule over thine house, having thy bridal bed as carrying dowry with it? I must in that case have been a fool, and not at all in my senses. But did I do it as though to reign were pleasant to the modest? By no means indeed is it, except monarchy have destroyed the minds of men who are pleased with her. But I would wish indeed to be first victor in the Grecian games, but second in the state ever to be happy with the most excellent friends. For thus is it possible to be well circumstanced: but the absence of the danger gives greater joy than dominion. One of my arguments has not been spoken, but the rest you are in possession of: for, if I had a witness such as myself am, and were she alive during my contention, you would know the evil ones, searching them by their works. But now I swear by Jove, the guardian of oaths, and by the plain of the earth, that never touched I thy bridal bed, nor ever wished it, nor conceived the thought. Else may I perish inglorious, without a name, and may neither sea nor earth receive the flesh of me when dead, if I be a wicked man. But whether or no she have destroyed her life through fear, I know not: for it is not lawful for me to speak further. Cautious she was, though she could not be chaste; but I, who could be, had the power to no good purpose.

CHORUS

Thou hast said sufficient to rebut the charge, in offering the oaths by the Gods, no slight proof.

THESEUS

Is not this man then an enchanter and a juggler, who trusts that he will overcome my mind by his goodness of disposition, after he has dishonored his father?

HIPPOLYTUS

I too very much wonder at this conduct of yours, my father; for if you were my son, and I your father, I should slay you, and not punish you by banishment, if you had dared to defile my wife.

THESEUS

How fitly hast thou said this! yet thou shalt not so die, as thou hast laid down this law for thyself; for a quick grave is easiest to the miserable man; but wandering an exile from thy country's land to foreign realms, thou shalt drag out a life of bitterness; for this is the reward for the impious man.

HIPPOLYTUS

Ah me! what wilt thou do? wilt thou not even await time as evidence against me, but wilt thou banish me from the land?

THESEUS

Ay, beyond the ocean, and the place of Atlas, if any way I could, so much do I hate thee.

HIPPOLYTUS

Without having even examined oath, or proof, or the sayings of the seers, wilt thou cast me uncondemned from out the land?

THESEUS

This letter here, that waiteth no seer's observations, accuses thee faithfully; but to the birds that flit above my head I bid a long farewell.

HIPPOLYTUS

O Gods, wherefore then do I not ope my mouth, who am destroyed by you whom I worship?—And yet not so—for thus I should not altogether persuade those whom I ought, but should be violating to no purpose the oaths which I have sworn.

THESEUS

Alas me! how thy sanctity kills me! Wilt not thou go as quick as possible from thy country's land?

HIPPOLYTUS

Whither then shall I unhappy turn me; what stranger's mansion shall I enter, banished on this charge?

THESEUS

His, who delights to entertain defilers of women, and those who dwell with evil deeds.

HIPPOLYTUS

Alas! alas! this goes to my heart, and almost makes me weep: if indeed I appear vile, and seem so to thee.

THESEUS

Then oughtest thou to have groaned, and owned the guilt before, when thou daredst to wrong thy father's wife.

HIPPOLYTUS
O mansions, would that ye could utter me a voice, and bear witness whether I be a vile man!

THESEUS
Dost fly to dumb witnesses? this deed, though it speak not, clearly proves thee vile.

HIPPOLYTUS
Alas! would that I could look upon myself standing opposite, to that degree do I weep for the evils which I suffer!

THESEUS
Thou hast accustomed thyself much more to regard thyself, than to be a just man, and to do what is righteous to thy parents.

HIPPOLYTUS
O unhappy mother! O wretched natal hour! may none of my friends ever be illegitimate.

THESEUS
Servants, will ye not drag him out? did you not hear me long ago pronounce him banished!

HIPPOLYTUS
Any one of them shall touch me to his cost however; but thou thyself, if it be thy desire, thrust me out from the land.

THESEUS
I will do this, unless thou wilt obey my words, for no pity for thy banishment comes over me.

HIPPOLYTUS
It is fixed, as it seems; alas, wretch that I am! since I know these things indeed, but know not how to say them. O most dear to me of deities, daughter of Latona, thou that assortest with me, huntest with me, we shall then indeed be banished illustrious Athens: but farewell O city, and land of Erectheus. O plain of Trœzene, how many things hast thou to employ the happy youth! Farewell! for I address thee, beholding thee for the last time—Come youths of this land my companions, bid me farewell, and conduct me from the land, for never shall you see a man more chaste, even though I seem not to my father.

CHORUS
Surely the providence of the Gods, when it comes into my mind, greatly takes away sorrow: but cherishing in my hope some knowledge, I am utterly deficient, when I look on the fortunes and on the deeds of men, for they are changed in different manners, and the life of man varies, ever exceeding vague. Would that in answer to my petitions fate from the Gods would give me this, prosperity with riches, and a mind unsullied by griefs. And be my character neither too high, nor on the other hand infamous. But changing my easy habits with the morrow ever may I lead a happy life; for no longer have I an unperturbed mind, but I see things contrary to my expectations: since we have seen the brightest star of Grecian Minerva sent forth to another land on account of his father's rage. O sands of the neighboring shore, and mountain wood, where with the swift-footed dogs he wont to slay the wild beasts, accompanying the chaste Dian! No more shalt thou mount the car drawn by the team of Henetian steeds, restraining with thy foot the horses in their exercise on the

course round Limna. And the sleepless song that used to dwell under the bridge of the chords shall cease in thy father's house. And the haunts of the daughter of Latona in the deep wood shall be without their garlands: and the contest among the damsels for thy bridal bed has died away by reason of thy exile. But I, for thy misfortunes, shall endure with tears a fortuneless fortune. O unhappy mother, thou hast brought forth in vain! Alas! I am enraged with the Gods. Alas! alas! united charms of marriage, wherefore send ye the unhappy one, guilty of no crime, away from his country's land—away from these mansions?

But lo! I perceive a follower of Hippolytus with a sad countenance coming toward the house in haste.

MESSENGER, CHORUS.

MESSENGER
Ye females, whither going can I find Theseus, king of this land? If ye know, tell me: is he within this palace?

CHORUS
The king himself is coming out of the palace.

MESSENGER, THESEUS, CHORUS.

MESSENGER
I bring a tale that demands concern, of thee and of thy subjects, both those who inhabit the city of the Athenians, and the realms of the Trœzenian land.

THESEUS
What is it? Has any sudden calamity come upon the two neighboring states?

MESSENGER
To speak the word—Hippolytus is no more. He views the light however for a short moment.

THESEUS
Killed? By whom? Has any come to enmity with him, whose wife, as his father's, he has forcibly defiled?

MESSENGER
His own chariot slew him, and the imprecations of thy mouth, which thou didst put up to thy father, the ruler of the ocean, concerning thy son.

THESEUS
O ye Gods! and O Neptune! how truly then wert thou my father, when thou didst duly hear my imprecations! Tell me too, how did he perish? in what way did the staff of Justice strike him that disgraced me?

MESSENGER
We indeed near the wave-beaten shore were combing out with combs the horses' hair, weeping, for there had come a messenger saying, that Hippolytus no longer trod on this land, having from thee received the sentence of wretched banishment. But he came bringing to us on the shore the same strain of tears: and an innumerable throng of his friends and companions came following with him. But at length after some time he spake, having ceased from his groans. "Wherefore am I thus

disquieted? My father's words must be obeyed. My servants, yoke to my car the harnessed steeds, for this city is for me no more." Then indeed every man hasted, and sooner than one could speak we drew up the horses caparisoned before our master; and he seizes with his hands the reins from off the bow of the chariot, mounting with his foot sandaled as it was. And first indeed he addressed the Gods with outstretched hands: "Jove, may I no longer exist, if I am a base man; but may my father perceive how unworthily he treats me, either when I am dead, or while I view the light." And on this having taken the whip in his hands he struck the horses both at once: and we the attendants followed our master by the chariot close to the reins, along the road that leads straightway to Argos and Epidauria, but when we came into the desert country, there is a certain shore beyond this land which slopes even down to the Saronic Sea, from thence a voice like the subterraneous thunder of Jove sent forth a dreadful groan appalling to hear, and the horses pointed their heads erect and their ears toward the sky, and on us there came a vehement fear, whence possibly the voice could come: but looking toward the sea-beaten shore we beheld a vast wave pillared in heaven, so that the view of the heights of Sciron was taken from mine eye: and it concealed the Isthmus and the rock of Æsculapius. And then swelling up and splashing forth much foam around in the ocean surf, it moves toward the shore, where was the chariot drawn by its four horses. But together with its breaker and its tripled surge, the wave sent forth a bull, a fierce monster; with whose bellowing the whole land filled resounded fearfully: and to the lookers-on a sight appeared more dreadful than the eyes could bear. And straightway a dreadful fear comes over the steeds. But their master, being much conversant with the ways of horses, seized the reins in his hands, and pulls them as a sailor pulls his oar, having fixed his body in an opposite direction to the reins. But they, champing with their jaws the forged bits, bare him on forcibly, heeding neither the hand that steered them, nor the traces, nor the compact chariot: and, if indeed holding the reins he directed their course toward the softer ground, the bull appeared in front, so as to turn them away maddening with fright the four horses that drew the chariot. But if they were borne to the rocks maddened in mettle, silently approaching the chariot he followed so far, until he overthrew it and drove it backward, dashing the felly of the wheel against the rock. And all was in confusion, and the naves of the wheels flew up, and the linch-pins of the axles. But the unhappy man himself entangled in the reins is dragged along, bound in a difficult bond, his head dashed against the rocks, and torn his flesh, and crying out in a voice dreadful to hear, "Stop, O ye that have been trained up in my stalls, do not destroy me. Oh unhappy imprecation of my father! Who will come near and save a most excellent man?" But many of us wishing so to do failed through want of swiftness: and he indeed freed, in what manner I know not, from the entanglements of the reins, falls, having the breath of life in him, but for a very short time. And the horses vanished, and the woeful monster of the bull I know not where in the mountain country. I am indeed the slave of thy house, O king, but thus much never shall I at least be able to be persuaded of thy son, that he is evil, not even if the whole race of women were hung, and though one should fill with writing all the fir of Ida, since I am confident that he is virtuous.

CHORUS
Alas! alas! The calamity of new evils is consummated, nor is there refuge from fate and from what must be.

THESEUS
Through hate of the man, who has thus suffered, I was pleased with this account; but now, having respect unto the Gods, and to him, because he is of me, I am neither pleased, nor yet troubled at these ills.

MESSENGER
How then? Must we bring him hither, or what must we do to the unhappy man to gratify thy wishes! Think; but if thou take my advice, thou wilt not be harsh toward thy son in his misfortunes.

THESEUS

Bear him hither, that seeing him before my eyes that denied he had defiled my bed, I may confute him with words, and with what has happened from the Gods.

CHORUS

Thou, Venus, bendest the stubborn mind of the Gods, and of mortals, and with thee he of varied plume, that darts about on swiftest wing; and flies over the earth and over the loud-resounding briny ocean; and Love charms to subjection, on whose maddened heart the winged urchin come gleaming with gold, the race of the mountain whelps, and of those that inhabit the sea, and as many things as the earth nourisheth, which the sun doth behold scorched with its rays, and men: but over all these things thou, Venus, alone holdest sovereign rule.

DIANA, THESEUS, CHORUS.

DIANA

Thee, the noble son of Ægeus, I command to listen; but it is I, Diana, daughter of Latona, who am addressing thee: Theseus, wherefore dost thou, wretched man, take delight in these things, seeing that thou hast slain in no just way thy son, being persuaded by the lying words of thy wife in things not seen? But the guilt that has seized on thee is manifest. How canst thou, shamed as thou art, refrain from hiding thy body beneath the dark recesses of the earth? or from withdrawing thy foot from this suffering, by changing thy nature, and becoming a winged creature above? Since among good men at least thou hast not a part in life to possess. Hear, O Theseus, the state of thy ills. Even though I gain no advantage from it, yet will I torment thee; but for this purpose came I to show thee the upright mind of thy son, that he may die with a good reputation, and thy wife's passion, or, in some sort, nobleness; for, gnawed by the stings of that deity most hateful to us, as many as delight in virginity, she became enamored of thy son. But while she endeavored by right feeling to conquer Venus, she was destroyed not willingly by the means employed by the nurse, who having first bound him by oaths, told thy son her malady. But he, as was right, obeyed not her words; nor, again, though evil-entreated by thee, did he violate the sanctity of his oaths, being a pious man. But she, fearing lest her conduct should be scrutinized, wrote a false letter, and by deceit destroyed thy son, but nevertheless persuaded thee.

THESEUS

Ah me!

DIANA

My tale torments thee, Theseus, but be still, that having heard what follows thou mayest groan the more—Knowest thou then that thou receivedst from thy father three wishes with a certainty of their being granted? Whereof one thou hast expended, O most evil one, on thy son, when thou mightest have done it on some of thine enemies. Thy father then that dwelleth in the ocean, gave thee as much as he was bound to give, because he promised. But thou both in his eyes and in mine appearest evil, who neither didst await nor examine proof, nor the voice of the prophets, didst not leave the consideration to length of time, but, quicker than became thee, didst vent thy curses against thy son and slay him.

THESEUS

Mistress, let me die!

DIANA

Thou hast committed dreadful deeds, but nevertheless, it is still possible even for thee to obtain pardon for these things. For Venus willed that these things should be in order to satiate her rage. But among the Gods the law is thus—None wishes to thwart the purpose of him that wills anything, but we always give way. Since, be well assured, were it not that I feared Jove, never should I have come to such disgrace, as to suffer to die a man of all mortals the most dear to me. But thine error, first of all thine ignorance frees from malice; and then thy wife by her dying put an end to the proof of words, so as to persuade thy mind. Chiefly then on thee these ills are burst, but sorrow is to me too; for Gods rejoice not when the pious die; the wicked however we destroy with their children and their houses.

CHORUS
And lo! the unhappy man there is coming, all mangled his young flesh and auburn head. Oh the misery of the house! such double anguish coming down from heaven has been wrought in the palaces!

HIPPOLYTUS, DIANA, THESEUS, CHORUS.

HIPPOLYTUS
O! O! O! Unhappy I was thus foully mangled by the unjust prayers of an unjust father—I am destroyed miserably. Ah me! ah me! Pains rush through my head, and the spasm darts across my brain. Stop, I will rest my fainting body. Oh! oh! O those hateful horses of my chariot, things which I fed with my own hand, ye have destroyed me utterly and slain me. Oh! oh! by the Gods, gently, my servants, touch with your hands my torn flesh. Who stands by my side on the right? Lift me up properly, and take hold all equally on me, the unblessed of heaven, and cursed by my father's error—Jove, Jove, beholdest thou these things? Lo! I, the chaste, and the reverencer of the Gods, I who in modesty exceed all, have lost my life, and go to a manifest hell beneath the earth; but in vain have I labored in the task of piety toward men. O! O! O! and now the pain, the pain comes upon me, loose unhappy me, and let death come to be my physician. Destroy me, destroy the unhappy one—I long for a two-edged blade, wherewith to cut me in pieces, and to put my life to an eternal rest. Oh unhappy curse of my father! the evil too of my blood-polluted kinsmen, my old forefathers, bursts forth upon me; nor is it at a distance; and it hath come on me, wherefore, I pray, who am nothing guilty of these ills? Alas me! me! what can I say? how can I free my life from this cruel calamity? Would that the black and nightly fate of Pluto would put me wretched to eternal sleep!

DIANA
Oh unhappy mortal, with what a calamity art thou enthralled! but the nobleness of thy mind hath destroyed thee.

HIPPOLYTUS
Let be. O divine breathing of perfume, for, even though being in ills, I perceived thee, and felt my body lightened of its pain. The Goddess Dian is in this place.

DIANA
Oh unhappy one! she is, to thee the most dear of deities.

HIPPOLYTUS
Mistress, thou seest wretched me, in what state I am.

DIANA
I see; but it is not lawful for me to shed a tear down mine eyes.

HIPPOLYTUS
Thy hunter, and thy servant is no more.

DIANA

No in sooth; but beloved by me thou perishest.

HIPPOLYTUS

And he that managed they steeds, and guarded thy statutes.

DIANA

Ay, for the crafty Venus hath so wrought.

HIPPOLYTUS

Ah me! I perceive indeed the power that hath destroyed me.

DIANA

She thought her honor aggrieved, and hated thee for being chaste.

HIPPOLYTUS

One Venus hath destroyed us three.

DIANA

Thy father, and thee, and his wife the third.

HIPPOLYTUS

I mourn therefore also my father's misery.

DIANA

He was deceived by the devices of the Goddess.

HIPPOLYTUS

Oh! unhappy thou, because of this calamity, my father!

THESEUS

I perish, my son, nor have I delight in life.

HIPPOLYTUS

I lament thee rather than myself on account of thy error.

THESEUS

My son, would that I could die in thy stead!

HIPPOLYTUS

Oh! the bitter gifts of thy father Neptune!

THESEUS

Would that the prayer had never come into my mouth.

HIPPOLYTUS

Wherefore this wish? thou wouldst have slain me, so enraged wert thou then.

THESEUS

For I was deceived in my notions by the Gods.

HIPPOLYTUS
Alas! would that the race of mortals could curse the Gods!

DIANA
Let be; for not even when thou art under the darkness of the earth shall the rage arising from the bent of the Goddess Venus descend upon thy body unrevenged: by reason of thy piety and thy excellent mind. For with these inevitable weapons from mine own hand will I revenge me on another, whoever to her be the dearest of mortals. But to thee, O unhappy one, in recompense for these evils, will I give the greatest honors in the land of Trœzene; for the unwedded virgins before their nuptials shall shear their locks to thee for many an age, owning the greatest sorrow tears can give; but ever among the virgins shall there be a remembrance of thee that shall awake the song, nor dying away without a name shall Phædra's love toward thee pass unrecorded:—But thou, O son of the aged Ægeus, take thy son in thine arms and clasp him to thee; for unwillingly thou didst destroy him, but that men should err, when the Gods dispose events, is but to be expected!—and thee, Hippolytus, I exhort not to remain at enmity with thy father; for thou perceivest the fate, whereby thou wert destroyed. And farewell! for it is not lawful for me to behold the dead, nor to pollute mine eye with the gasps of the dying; but I see that thou art now near this calamity.

HIPPOLYTUS
Go thou too, and farewell, blessed virgin! But thou easily quittest a long companionship. But I give up all enmity against my father at thy request, for before also I was wont to obey thy words. Ah! ah! darkness now covers me over mine eyes. Take hold on me, my father, and lift up my body.

THESEUS
Ah me! my son, what dost thou, do to me unhappy?

HIPPOLYTUS
I perish, and do indeed see the gates of hell.

THESEUS
What? leaving my mind uncleansed from thy blood?

HIPPOLYTUS
No in sooth, since I free thee from this murder.

THESEUS
What sayest thou? dost thou remit me free from the guilt of blood?

HIPPOLYTUS
I call to witness Dian that slays with the bow.

THESEUS
O most dear, how noble thou appearest to thy father!

HIPPOLYTUS
O farewell thou too, take my best farewell, my father!

THESEUS
Oh me! for thy pious and brave soul!

HIPPOLYTUS

Pray to have legitimate sons like me.

THESEUS

Do not, I prithee, leave me, my son, but be strong.

HIPPOLYTUS

My time of strength is past; for I perish, my father: but cover my face as quickly as possible with robes.

THESEUS

O famous realms of Athens and of Pallas, of what a man will ye have been bereaved! Oh unhappy I! What abundant reason, Venus, shall I have to remember thy ills!

CHORUS

This common grief to all the citizens hath come unexpectedly. There will be a fast falling of many tears; for the mournful stories of great men rather obtain.

www.ingramcontent.com/pod-product-compliance
Lightning Source LLC
Chambersburg PA
CBHW060141050426
42448CB00010B/2244